SUPER
OWNERSHIP

How School **Superintendents** Can Elevate K–12 Systems

JOHN BARRY

SuperOwnership Consulting

Published byEduVision

SuperOwnership
Consulting

Produced by GMK Writing and Editing, Inc.
Managing Editor: Katie Benoit
Cover and text design by Vicky Vaughn Shea
Composition by Joanna Beyer
Copyedited by Amy Paradysz
Proofread by Elizabeth Crooks

Print ISBN: 978-1-966981-13-8
Ebook EISN: 978-1-966981-14-5

Visit the author at SuperOwnership.com

This work was written, designed, and produced without the use of AI (Artificial Intelligence). Human creativity and intelligence may not be perfect, but they are far better than anything artificial.

*To every superintendent who believes that ownership
is not just a duty but a calling—may this book
inspire your leadership and light your path.*

Acknowledgments

So many people contributed their time, energy, and insight to help bring this book to life. First and foremost, I want to express my deepest appreciation to the educators, school leaders, support personnel, and board members who continue—day in and day out—to shape the future of our public education system. You are the heroes of this story. Your commitment to students, families, and communities is what makes transformation possible. Super Ownership was written for you and because of you.

As the book took shape, I had the privilege of speaking with many colleagues and friends—inside and outside the education world—who offered feedback, encouragement, and critical reflection. While I cannot name everyone here, please know that your contributions were essential, and I am profoundly grateful for your support and candor.

I want to extend my deepest gratitude to the entire Aurora Public Schools team whose dedication and spirit made our journey such a success. Many of you gave precious time from already full schedules to share your stories, insights, and challenges. Your contributions not only shaped the work we accomplished together but also enriched its meaning for future superintendents and education leaders. You gave more than was ever asked, and for that, I will remain forever thankful. Special thanks to Tony Van Gytenbeek, William Stuart, Lisa Escarcega, Cheryl Dalton, Geogia Duran, Anthony Sturges, Rod Weeks, Kari Allen, Tammy Clementi, Brian Donovan, Kathleen Hostetler, Sue Clark, Matt Cook, Julie-Marie Shepherd, Judy Edberg, Dan Jorgensen, and Linda Bowman.

I am grateful to Tim Quinn and Shelley Keith, whose mentorship as directors of the Broad Superintendent Academy shaped my superintedent leadership. Tim—who recently passed—challenged me to lead with courage and clarity; his example lives on in these pages. Shelley's steady counsel and encouragement anchored my growth.

I am deeply grateful to my book producer, Gary Krebs, whose steady patience, wise counsel, and unwavering belief in this book carried me through each stage of its creation. My thanks as well to my editor, Katie Benoit, whose discerning insights and sharp editorial eye refined the message and lifted the work to a higher plane.

Finally, and most importantly, I owe an immeasurable debt of gratitude to my family. To Ellen, my devoted wife—your patience, generosity, and grace sustained me through the countless late nights, early mornings, and weekends devoted to this work. You surrendered time together so that I might give voice to these pages, and your steadfast support has been the quiet strength behind every word. To my children, whose lives and accomplishments fill me with enduring pride, and to our eight beloved grandchildren—may your journeys be as richly blessed as the joy you have bestowed upon mine.

To everyone who walked this journey with me—educators, leaders, friends, readers, and champions of public education—thank you.

—John Barry

Contents

Prologue...xiii
Introduction...xvii
Executive Summary...xxi

Part One: Internal Transformation
Chapter One: Transitioning to Public Education 3
Chapter Two: Starting with Listening....................................17
Chapter Three: Owning the Case for a Transformation...............29
Chapter Four: Earning and Owning Credibility 49
Chapter Five: Owning and Orchestrating a Transformation 71
Chapter Six: Owning Inputs and Outputs 95

Part Two: External Transformation
Chapter Seven: Generating Community Ownership...................109
Chapter Eight: Owning the Need for External Learning
    Opportunities 127
Chapter Nine: Owning Crisis Management....................................149

Part Three: Putting It All Together
Chapter Ten: Cultivating Ownership in Transforming K-12
    Education 163
Chapter Eleven: Modeling Leadership...199
Chapter Twelve: Key Insights and Takeaways 223

APPENDIX A: Superintendent Ninety-Day Listening Tour......229
APPENDIX B: Ninety-Day Entry Plan, Goals,
    and Objectives 233
APPENDIX C: Ninety-Day Stakeholder Interviews
    and Timelines... 241

APPENDIX D: Incident Response Team Checklists 257

APPENDIX E: Resources 273

About the Author: John Barry 277

Prologue

I once considered titling this book *No One Washes a Rented Car*—a nod to the idea that people take care of what they truly own. The phrase captures a fundamental truth: Ownership drives investment, pride, and performance. But as this work evolved, it became clear that the concept of ownership in education—particularly for superintendents—deserved a title that fully reflected both the gravity of the responsibility and the transformative potential of true leadership.

Super Ownership speaks to the kind of bold, authentic, and accountable leadership required to elevate K-12 systems. This book is about what happens when superintendents embrace their roles with a deeper sense of responsibility—fostering both internal and external transformation that benefits students, strengthens communities, and shapes the future of public education.

Ownership is a consistent theme in this book as it serves as a basic insight into the need for American citizens and our students to own K-12 education. For adults involved in education, we need to own the importance of public education for two reasons: (1) For us to maintain leadership in the world economically, politically, and militarily, we must ensure our next generation maximizes its potential academically; and (2) Our children will not compete for jobs in just our cities, our states, or even in our nation; they will compete for jobs globally, and they have to be prepared.

If you have any doubt about this, consider the following:

- The United States of America has 50 million K-12 students. China and India combined have a total of approximately 515 million students. If you just do the math, the top 10 percent of these two countries alone comes close to equaling the total number of students we have in all of our elementary, middle, and high schools. There are students in the world who will challenge the next generation's Steve Jobs, Bill Gates, and Warren Buffett.
- The internet has opened the world to almost every person on this planet. Harvard University, Yale University, and Duke University, just to name a few, are offering free college-level core courses online worldwide.
- In his book *The Great Convergence: Asia, the West, and the Logic of One World,* Singaporean diplomat Kishore Mahbubani says there are 500 million Asians who enjoy middle-class living standards today but by 2020 there will be 1.75 billion, an increase of three and a half times. With that many people gaining a higher socio-economic status, there are going to be more educated competitors on the global scene.

We need to ignite the passion for learning in every young person in our country. By offering choices in subject areas of interest as early as elementary school, more focused options in middle school, and clearly targeted options in high school, we can create ownership of those choices in areas of interest that will drive motivation. When I was a student in K-12 schools in the 1950s and 1960s, we graduated from high school with the same diploma and almost all the same graduation credit requirements. In that twentieth-century model of education, we could finally declare a major and enter studies in content areas of our interest in our second year of college. In the twenty-first century, we need to solicit passion in our students at the earliest age possible.

To prepare our students for global competition and be globally relevant, our entire community of districts, counties, cities, and states must "own" the process, procedures, and pedagogy of public education—not just leave it to the educators in our schools.

Choice equals ownership and ownership equals motivation. That is why "no one ever washes a rented car." We need to own the education of our nation's students, *internally as educators and externally as communities*, to purposefully raise the leadership effectiveness and the concepts of twenty-first century learning to allow the United States to be globally competitive in K-12 and higher education.

Complex Problems Require Complex Solutions

Success is rarely the result of a single action; success comes from multiple initiatives that allow students, parents, and staff to find the right path for them. Ownership equals motivation, which is why it is critical to develop, encourage, and support new definitions of what school is and can be.

An organization can be structured to advance and succeed, but it takes more than good intentions, vision, open and honest conversations, and enlightened attitudes. While these are essential elements, transformation also demands good structural design work that ties the parts together. The design must be responsive to the students and community the district serves. There is no cookie-cutter solution. Leadership that is distributive and inclusive can create a synergy for success. School districts can benefit and learn from the experience of others, but, in the end, each school district must find its own way.

This book shares my experience as a nontraditional educator who had the privilege to work in K-12 education, bringing to bear executive leadership skills learned in the military and private sectors. I chose a blend of personal narrative and instructional guidance to provide context for the ideas presented and to help you connect the principles of ownership and transformation to real-world leadership challenges. By sharing my journey alongside strategies and practices, I hope to make the lessons more relatable, actionable, and meaningful as you work to elevate your own educational communities. I trust the insights shared will be useful to you in your work transforming our educational systems to meet the challenges of the twenty-first century. Superintendents who own their mission don't just change schools—they change lives, communities, and the course of history.

Introduction

It was early in the morning on July 20, 2012 when I was awoken by my ringing phone. I had many phone calls at odd hours over a thirty-year career in the military but few during the seven years I served as superintendent of a large urban school district. As I shook the blanket of sleep from my eyes, I was informed by our school district's chief operating officer that there had been a shooting at a local movie theater and they needed help in opening a high school as a place to take witnesses of the crime.

The reality quickly set in, and I had flashbacks of being in the Pentagon on 9/11 and being in combat as a commander/fighter pilot flying over Iraq. I was struck by the confluence of the crises I experienced in the military—and now in a city I called home in my own country.

As I struggled to get initial information—which, based on my history in crisis situations, I knew would be 80 percent wrong—I agreed to assist immediately in opening Gateway High School for whatever was needed. I knew this was going to be a long day and made plans to assemble our school district Incident Response Team (IRT), a team that we had trained scores of times over six years in emergency simulations and minor school incidents.

As the phone calls started coming in, it was evident our IRT would play a major support role for the first responders on the scene. Media outlets from around Colorado and the nation were busily trying to report what was happening. I knew the media could be a valuable resource in assessing initial situations in civilian events, something we were never guaranteed of in the military when fighting wars in other countries. The TV and internet were awash with floods of video and interviews as media reporters responded to the shooting and reported what they knew regarding the who, what, where, when, and how—the questions you must start working on as soon as possible, while recognizing that the fog of a crisis will blanket the facts with great uncertainty.

While this was not a shooting in one of our schools, the impact would resonate throughout the city and directly impact our fall opening of school in two weeks. I knew immediately that this tragedy was developing into a calamity that would affect our nation, the state of Colorado, and the role of our school district in performing our primary duty in accelerating student achievement. The issues of safety, security, and recovery of our 40,000 students and over 4,500 staff members would now be a primary focus of our efforts for months to come.

Here was a convergence of realities and life experiences that I knew would have long-time impacts and consequences. It would compel me to examine the lessons learned in my careers as a retired Major General in the United States Air Force, a vice president of an international corporation, and the superintendent of the sixth-largest school district in Colorado. I had other crisis experiences in the past that had caused me to be introspective, and the theater shooting in Aurora provided a new cause for reflection.

While reflecting on this tragedy, I recalled the many times I had been asked what surprised me the most about K-12 education, since I was a nontraditional educator who came to the education field for the first time at the age of fifty-five. It is easy to give short and snarky answers to that question ("My staff don't salute me; they don't call me General"). But upon reflection, I realized that the leadership knowledge and experience I had acquired in the military, business, education, and nonprofit sectors could be positively applied in the work of regaining global leadership in public education. Witnessing this tragic event reminded me that life is short and that it was time for me to share what I had learned by writing this book.

Why does this matter to you, the reader? Because the challenges facing K-12 education today are larger than any single classroom, school, or district. If you are a superintendent, principal, or policymaker, you already know the weight of expectation: raise student outcomes, rebuild trust, prepare young people for a raplidly changing workforce, and do it all under intense public scrutiny. Managing alone is no longer enough—true leadership requires transformation.

This book is divided into two major sections: Internal Transformation and External Transformation. The theory of action is simple but urgent: K–12 education cannot meet the challenges of the twenty-first century unless leaders own both. Internal transformation strengthens schools from within, but without external transformation—engaging parents, communities, and the workforce—progress will stall. Too many conversations stop at internal bureaucracy; this book goes further, showing how schools and communities together can assume ownership of a shared future.

Drawing on my experience as a nontraditional educator, I share practical lessons learned in creating both internal and external ownership—insights that can help you lead with clarity and achieve lasting results.

- The only leadership book focused on both internal and external transformation of K–12 school districts.
- A framework for achieving early wins while sustaining long-term systemic reform.
- Strategies for fostering ownership at every level— from teachers and students to parents and community leaders.
- A blueprint for aligning schools with America's future workforce and civic needs.
- Particularly valuable for new K–12 superintendents and state commissioners of education who must lead change from day one.

Executive Summary

This book chronicles a bold and effective transformation of a K-12 school district led by a nontraditional superintendent. Rooted in urgency, strategic planning, community collaboration, and relentless execution, the transformation provides a blueprint that other districts can replicate by embracing ownership, data-driven decisions, and a commitment to outcomes. The following are the key steps and phases critical to replicating this transformation:

1. Own the Need for Change

Recognize and openly acknowledge the need for transformation. Assess the current state of the district through data and stakeholder feedback, identifying gaps in student achievement, operations, and equity.

2. Apply a Change Leadership Model

Use a proven framework such as John Kotter's 8-Step Change Model to guide your transformation journey. Start by creating a sense of urgency, building coalitions, and articulating a compelling vision.

3. Establish Clear Vision and Mission

Redefine your district's purpose around student outcomes, workforce readiness, and twenty-first-century skills. Communicate this vision consistently and compellingly to all stakeholders.

4. Show Early Results ("Quick Wins")

Prioritize initiatives that can generate measurable improvements within the first 6–12 months. This builds credibility, gains buy-in, and reinforces the belief that change is possible.

5. Gain Champions for Key Initiatives

Identify and empower high-capacity principals, teachers, and community leaders who will serve as champions of change. Use data and storytelling to build their advocacy.

6. Shift from Inputs to Outcomes

Refocus the district's attention from traditional process-oriented measures (like hours taught or compliance) to student-centered outcomes such as achievement, attendance, and graduation rates.

7. Build Strategic External Partnerships

Engage businesses, higher education, civic groups, and non-profits to align educational goals with community needs. These partnerships should enhance learning, internships, and workforce pipelines.

8. Implement External Learning Opportunities (ELOs)

Create and scale real-world learning experiences—such as job shadows, internships, and apprenticeships—that connect students to future careers and reinforce the relevance of their education.

9. Embed Ownership at All Levels

Foster a culture where students, staff, families, and the community share ownership of educational success. Develop structures and incentives that promote responsibility and accountability.

10. Lead with Transparency and Communication

Establish strong internal and external communications strategies. Use clear, consistent messaging and multiple platforms to share progress, challenges, and next steps.

11. Institutionalize Crisis Management Practices

Develop and regularly exercise a district-wide Incident Response Team (IRT). Collaborate with city agencies to prepare for and manage crises, ensuring student safety and system resilience.

12. Focus on Talent—Hiring, Retention, and Evaluation

Refine recruitment and retention strategies to ensure high-quality staff. Shift evaluation systems to prioritize impact on student outcomes rather than solely on instructional methods.

13. Address Equity Systemically

Embed equity into every phase of transformation. Disaggregate data to uncover gaps, then design and fund targeted interventions to eliminate disparities in learning and opportunity.

14. Build Capacity for Sustained Innovation

Invest in leadership development, adaptive systems, and scalable models. Avoid one-off initiatives; instead, focus on long-term capacity building that fosters a culture of continuous improvement.

15. Learn, Reflect, and Adapt

Institutionalize a cycle of reflection through regular "hot washes" (post-initiative debriefs), stakeholder feedback loops, and data reviews. Adjust strategies as needed to ensure ongoing relevance and impact.

By following these steps and owning every phase of the transformation, districts can move from complacency to excellence—empowering all students to thrive in today's rapidly changing world.

PART ONE

Internal Transformation

CHAPTER ONE

Transitioning to Public Education

The year 2003 promised to be a compelling year of celebration for the USAF since it was the 100-year anniversary of the Wright Brothers' flight at Kitty Hawk. By that time, I had been a pilot for almost thirty-two years, and I was excited about the pending celebrations. As a fighter pilot and often commander at the Squadron, Group, and Wing levels and reaching the rank of Major General in the USAF, I was scheduled to participate in many activities and give some speeches on how far we had come as a world, as a nation, and as a military service.

This excitement was shattered on February 1, 2003, when the world witnessed the sudden and profound loss of the space shuttle *Columbia* that killed all seven astronauts. While I had been the senior strategic planner for the USAF and had served as a White House Fellow in NASA during the *Challenger* space shuttle mishap in 1986, I was asked by the Chief of Staff of the Air Force, General John Jumper, to serve on the Investigation Board for the *Columbia* mishap.

The investigation was painful for the families of the seven crewmembers, the nation, and the world. Our board and contributing investigators worked tirelessly to develop credible findings and recommendations that were grounded in rigorous scientific and engineering principles. What the Columbia Accident Investigation Board concluded was that NASA had two causes for this accident. One was technical: a piece of foam, weighing 1.2 pounds, broke away from the external tank and impacted the left leading edge of the orbiter wing, causing a breach that allowed superheated air to penetrate the wing on re-entry, resulting in a breakup of *Columbia*.

The second cause was organizational: NASA had allowed cultural traits and organizational practices to develop that were detrimental to the safety of the organization.

This was a reflective time for me, and I found myself more and more intrigued by the study of large organizational failures. For personal reasons (and the fact that I had moved twenty-six times in over thirty years), I began to consider the possibility of retiring from the USAF, a family that I had been a part of since the age of seventeen when I entered the USAF Academy. I was honored to have served in the USAF, where the value of service above self became part of my life. It had been a privilege to help defend the great nation of the United States of America.

As it turned out, the *Columbia* investigation was to be my last assignment on active duty in the USAF. It was a compelling challenge that took nearly ten months to complete and ended with my serving as the Executive Director for the mishap investigation. After thirty years in the USAF, it was time to retire.

After leaving the Air Force, I was asked to speak on the lessons learned regarding the Columbia Accident Investigation and I continued to expand on my understandings of how large organizations fail. Increasingly, I was serving as a teacher of how complex organizations fail in complex ways. As a former student of public administration and with the opportunity to give speeches to nuclear power companies, aerospace companies, military war colleges, and public institutions, including K-12 and higher education, I was entering a new world of private and public institutions.

While I was in this phase of giving talks and speeches, I accepted a position with SAP, a German international corporation for industrial software. While I was a bit of a novice in international business, I found the experience exciting and challenging as I served as the vice president for Defense and Security. For nearly three years, I traveled the world—in one year, I traveled over 246,000 miles—and was introduced to the compelling challenges of education, business development, and solution management in countries in Europe and the Pacific. While I had visited many countries in my time in the USAF, these years boosted the number of nations I had visited or lived in to over sixty-five.

Working for SAP was insightful and extraordinary. I was impressed with the integrity of the company and I felt fortunate because of the opportunities it provided me in learning about the business world. However, the travel was wearing on me, and I knew there was something else I needed to do with my life.

One day, I received a notice in the mail about the Broad Superintendents Academy. Since I was used to receiving notices from various sources on prospective follow-on careers, I put it aside to look at some other time. Weeks later, while I was cleaning off my desk, I saw the letter again. I was curious now. The letter contained an offer to apply for a Broad Superintendent Fellowship. I had never heard of Broad, and I didn't know if it was even possible for someone with my background to be a superintendent of schools. I wasn't quite sure what a superintendent did.

The Broad Superintendents Academy was a leadership development program designed to train nontraditional candidates—often from military, business, or government backgrounds—to become school district superintendents. It was created by the Eli and Edythe Broad Foundation as part of its efforts to improve public education by applying private-sector strategies to school district management.

Unlike traditional superintendent training programs that primarily recruited career educators, the Broad Academy sought leaders from outside education, believing that strong leadership and management skills could drive large-scale improvement in urban school districts. Participants underwent rigorous training in areas such as finance, operations, data-driven decision-making, and human resources, with an emphasis on applying business and strategic management principles to education. The program targeted large (and often struggling) urban school districts where reform efforts were seen as most critical. Alumni of the program formed a network of leaders who shared strategies and best practices for transforming school systems. (The original Broad Superintendents Academy closed in 2014. However, its successor, the Broad Academy, was launched in partnership with Yale University's School of Management, continuing to train education leaders with a similar philosophy.)

As I researched the offer, I became more and more curious to understand the art of the possible regarding leadership in public education. I realized that many skill sets that I developed working in the USAF and with SAP, such as leadership, management, strategic planning, personnel management, and financial management, would be transferable if I were to lead a large school system. I also began to see a lot of commonality in my many experiences in command and the roles and responsibilities of running a school district. So, I applied.

As I went through the application process, I learned more and more about what it would mean to serve as a leader in public education. I read the book *Victory in Our Schools: We Can Give Our Children Excellent Public Education* by Major General John Stanford, USA (Ret.), who served as the superintendent of schools in Seattle from 1995 to 1998. He made a tremendous impact on the children in Seattle, and his leadership resulted in a tremendous turnaround. John Stanford served as a beacon for me in realizing the possibility of becoming a superintendent someday. In his book, he clearly shows how he deeply believed "every child can and must learn." His focus was always on accelerating student achievement and closing the achievement gaps regardless of adult issues that often got in the way. While I had served in the military and worked in the business world, I began to realize that my values aligned with the prospect of serving the next generation as an educator.

The Broad Superintendents Academy

While I was researching the fellowship, I became aware that Eli Broad, a billionaire from California, helped promote the hiring of former Colorado Governor Roy Romer (thirty-ninth governor of Colorado) to be the superintendent of the Unified School District in Los Angeles from 2001 to 2006. As part of that experience, Eli Broad initiated the Broad Superintendents Academy as an advanced development program that identifies and prepares experienced leaders from nontraditional professions to successfully run urban public education systems.

The more I learned about the Broad Superintendents Academy, the more it seemed to align with what I wanted to do with the next stage of my life. As I realized that my service in the USAF had given me the opportunity to help defend our nation, the prospect of being a superintendent became clearer as an opportunity to help defend the right of all children to learn. This philosophy is one that I realized I could embrace wholeheartedly, and I went forward with the application with renewed vigor.

I was fortunate to be selected in what turned out to be the third Broad Superintendents class, and those of us who were selected started our journey in January 2004. This fellowship is unique in a lot of ways. We met one Thursday-to-Sunday weekend every month for 10 months in a different city each time. While each session had specific goals, it gave us an opportunity to learn detailed information about the urban school district in the city that we were visiting. I worked as hard on this effort as I did for any of my degrees, even while still working for SAP. The fellowship confirmed that my skill sets were transferable and that the Broad Academy would fill in the gaps in my understandings of the nuances of K-12 education.

The staff from the Broad Academy was exceptional with the leadership of Shelley Keith and Tim Quinn—Tim had served as superintendent of the Green Bay Public Schools and served a term as Wisconsin's Deputy State Superintendent of Instruction. This team was able to bring in the best teachers, principals, superintendents, budget managers, curriculum experts, and even head-hunters who gave us advice on district application processes and experiences.

While I learned something new every day in my seven years as a superintendent, I felt the Broad Superintendents Academy served as a bridge in my understandings of urban education to the point where I felt comfortable enough to apply for a CEO position in an urban school district.

As I attended the monthly sessions at the Broad Superintendents Academy, I was struck by what surprised me. First, I was shocked at what I saw and studied regarding our country's public education system. In many cities I visited, there was a malaise among staff and teachers about what could be done for students in these urban school districts. One high school we visited in California had a metal detector, barbed wire around the perimeter of the school, pipes that were leaking, paint that was peeling, and a courtyard with a cafeteria that was too small for the student population and resulted in students eating outside as if they were in a prison yard.

I read *A Nation at Risk: The Imperative for Educational Reform*, the 1983 report of President Ronald Reagan's National Commission on Excellence in Education that described the dire state of our education system. While I read it with a sense of skepticism, it did open my eyes to a realization that our children needed a transformational educational system that would allow our country to enhance its global competitiveness. A spark of passion began burning in me to be a part of this noble effort. As I stated earlier, I had been privileged to help defend our nation with millions of others and I now saw the need to help defend the right of every child to learn.

Finding a Superintendent Role

I graduated from the Broad Superintendents Academy in December 2004. While I continued to meet my obligations at SAP, I was starting to research which school districts I could apply to as superintendent.

I was intrigued by how much power the different search firms had in developing a slate of candidates. When I was applying in the private sector for a job after retiring from the USAF, the executive search firms were catering to me as an individual when applying for a job to get the best position and salary—they advocated for me. In the K-12 world, the superintendent search firms had a lot of authority in recruiting, then selecting what slate of candidates to provide school districts—they advocated for the school district. Frankly, some of the search firms were of the opinion that nontraditional educators were not good fits for K-12 school districts so they didn't allow me to compete.

Fortunately, in 2006 I was able to be listed in a candidate pool for the Aurora Public Schools (APS) district in Colorado. This was a gift since I had always planned to return to Colorado. I graduated from the USAF Academy, my children attended college in Colorado, and I had owned mountain property near Steamboat Springs since 1973. To even be considered for a job in Colorado was a true godsend.

The selection process was arduous with many interviews with various stakeholders in the community, but it was fair. I was willing and able to join a school district like Aurora Public Schools that had the urban challenges of high poverty, growing student diversity, large English language-learner populations, and decreasing student achievement, similar to the challenges that I witnessed when I was in K-12 education as a student in the Bronx, New York. It was obvious that the Aurora community was a strong one that was committed to improving the opportunities for their children, but the student achievement was not improving. I was honored to be a candidate for the position of superintendent, and I was even more honored to be selected to serve the students of Aurora starting in July 2006.

KEY INSIGHTS FROM CHAPTER ONE
Transformational moments can redirect career paths.

- The Columbia Accident Investigation served as a pivotal experience, prompting deep reflection on organizational failure, leadership, and personal mission.
- Witnessing both technical and *organizational* causes of failure ignited a fascination with how large systems succeed—or break down.

Skills from military and business are transferable.

- Leadership, strategic planning, personnel management, and accountability—honed in the Air Force and at SAP—proved relevant and valuable in public education.
- My story challenges the idea that only career educators can lead school districts, promoting a broader view of leadership qualifications.

Nontraditional pathways can lead to deep educational impact.

- Through the Broad Superintendents Academy, I saw how cross-sector leadership experience could be a strength rather than a liability in transforming urban schools.
- The comparison between military command and school district leadership reframed public education leadership as a systems-based challenge, not just an instructional one.

A sense of service transcends sectors.

- Transitioning from defending the nation to defending the right of every child to learn created a sense of continuity in purpose.
- Public education leadership became an extension of lifelong public service—grounded in values rather than career progression.

Exposure to educational inequity sparked moral urgency.

- Firsthand visits to urban schools revealed conditions that mirrored institutional neglect and sparked a call to action.
- The contrast between military order and educational disarray added urgency to the mission of educational transformation.

Mentorship and inspiration can be powerful motivators.

- The example of Major General John Stanford, a fellow nontraditional superintendent, offered a compelling model of what impactful leadership could look like in education.
- His mantra—*every child can and must learn*—became a guiding principle for my journey.

Leadership development can bridge sector gaps.

- The Broad Academy provided essential context, tools, and networks to understand the nuances of education systems.
- Monthly immersive experiences and access to experienced educators helped fill knowledge gaps while building confidence and credibility.

Structural challenges exist in entering the K-12 field.

- The gatekeeping role of traditional superintendent search firms highlighted barriers faced by nontraditional candidates.
- Some firms dismissed candidates without educational pedigrees, reinforcing systemic resistance to change despite the potential of cross-sector leadership.

Where does your purpose align with place?

* Returning to Colorado—a place of personal and professional significance—offered a meaningful platform to implement lessons learned.
* Aurora's diverse, high-need population mirrored the very systems I hoped to help transform.

Leadership in public education is a complex, noble endeavor.

* The chapter frames superintendency not merely as a job but as a form of national service.
* My shift in identity—from general to educator—was rooted in a growing belief that transformational leadership could, and must, come from beyond the traditional mold.

CHAPTER QUESTIONS TO CONSIDER

1. **Personal Reflection:** How do you think your own experiences might influence your approach to leadership in a nontraditional career path?
2. **Organizational Learning:** What do you think are the key lessons learned from the Columbia Accident Investigation that could be applied to other large organizations, including educational institutions?
3. **Career Transition:** What challenges do you foresee in transitioning from a military or business career

to a role in public education? How might your previous experiences be an asset?

4. **Values and Motivation:** How do your personal values align with the idea of serving as a leader in public education? What drives you to consider such a significant career shift?

5. **Impact of Leadership:** In what ways do you believe leadership in the military or business can translate to leadership in a public school system? What skills or qualities are most transferable?

6. **Broad Superintendents Academy:** How do you think the Broad Superintendents Academy's focus on nontraditional candidates impacts the field of education? Do you think this approach is beneficial?

7. **Reflection on Public Education:** After learning about the state of public education described in this chapter, what do you believe are the most pressing challenges facing urban school districts today?

8. **Preparation for Leadership:** How would you prepare yourself to take on a leadership role in a field you are less familiar with? What steps would you take to ensure you are successful?

CHAPTER TWO

Starting with Listening

I had been serving as Superintendent for only a few months when I gained my first significant insight—one that any leader in education can apply. Drawing from my experience on the *Columbia* space shuttle accident investigation, I realized a truth that carried directly into my new school district: complex systems fail in complex ways, and they demand equally complex solutions. I came to realize that because there was no single reason why students do not succeed, no single solution could produce the results that were needed for a transformation. As a result, we would need to create a multifaceted, integrated strategic plan that would transform the entire school district.

Success is rarely the result of a single action. Success comes from multiple initiatives that allow students, parents, and staff to find the right path for them. An educational leader must believe that ownership equals motivation, and that is why it is critical to develop, encourage, and support new definitions of what schools can be. An organization can be structured to advance and succeed, but it takes more than good intentions, vision, open and honest conversations, and enlightened attitudes. While these are essential elements, a successful organization requires good structural design work that integrates the parts together.

The design, however, cannot be a hodgepodge of initiatives. It must be fully integrated and responsive to the students and community the district serves. There is no one solution or cookie-cutter solution. Leadership that is distributive and inclusive can create a synergy for success. School district leaders can benefit and learn from the experiences of others, though each district must find its own integrated strategy that matches its culture.

Leadership is the cornerstone of any successful transformation, and genuine leadership is not about racing ahead and hoping that others are following. Whether leading in the military, a business, a nonprofit, or a school district, I had learned from my own experience that it is better to lead by inspiring rather than commanding. I cannot help but think of Bruce Buchanan's words in his book *Turnover at the Top* when he said, "Today's urban school superintendent is expected to be a dynamic leader—someone who is part education expert, part CEO, and part tent revival preacher."

In every organization I have been a part of, I have learned that everyone wants and needs to understand the big picture before becoming engaged and supportive. In a school district, the first step for a superintendent is to make every stakeholder—the board of education, students, staff, parents, and the business community—believe that real change is possible and to unite around a strategic plan that has a common vision and mission. Sustainable leadership requires engaging all stakeholders. The next step is encouraging and building capacity for leadership that extends from the superintendent and board to every teacher and classroom as well as to students, parents, and the community.

Starting in August 2006, the board of education and I embarked on a ninety-day "listening tour" to learn what our stakeholders wanted and expected from APS. (My full listening tour outline—including what to do with staff, board, and community—is in Appendices A, B, and C.)

My approach to this ninety-day listening tour was different than what other new superintendents may have done. Typically, a new superintendent will spend the first ninety days meeting people and listening, then spend several months working with teams of stakeholders to develop a strategic plan. To me, the needs in Aurora were too great and this traditional approach was too slow.

Before interviewing for the position, I had already reviewed the district data. In 2006 it was obvious that the district had experienced dramatic changes in demographics. Within just six years, the percentage of English language learners had more than doubled to encompass nearly 40 percent of our student population. The number of students experiencing poverty had jumped from 35 percent to 64 percent. The district was overwhelmed and unable to adjust rapidly enough to its new student demographic, which was increasingly poor, increasingly mobile, and increasingly immigrant.

APS had some of the lowest state test scores in the Denver metropolitan area. Of all our schools, three out of four were rated low or unsatisfactory on the annual state report cards. Our students were well below the state levels for proficiency. We faced poor student achievement, poor attendance, and high dropout rates. The system was failing too many students and they were in a downward spiral for failure. Our own community had lost faith in the district. Continuing along the same route was a path to continued failure. Small adjustments and incremental changes would not be enough; a major change was needed. Meaningful change would only come from an integrated focus, not a hodgepodge of well-meaning initiatives. Too often, transformation in education is confused with acquiring the silver bullet, the supposedly single answer to the ills of public education—such as reorganizing a school or purchasing the latest curriculum or technological advancement. We needed a new approach.

Data confirms that students who start out below academic proficiency too often stay there. The three reasons most students drop out of school is as simple as A, B, C: **a**ttendance, **b**ehavior, or **c**redit deficiency. We decided that the best response to close the achievement gap and keep kids in school was to follow the three Rs: **r**igor, **r**elevancy, and **r**elationships.

To raise student achievement and close the achievement gaps among ethnic groups and economically diverse students, districts cannot afford to wait for individual schools to make changes on their own—they must create a clear vision and strong plan to enable and support every school within the system to be successful. You must find solutions to meet the challenges of poverty, transiency, language barriers, and disinterest. You need higher expectations and higher accountability for all. To restate a point for the reader, to raise student achievement and close the achievement gaps among ethnic groups and economically diverse students, each district needs a coherent vision, revitalized mission, and clearly focused strategic plan to address the district's current challenges and ensure a laser focus on student achievement.

As a new superintendent, I had an immediate and moral charge to raise student achievement and close the achievement gaps among ethnic and economically diverse students as soon as possible. Here are immediate examples of steps that you can take to foster the beginning of a transformation:

- Build on the district's transformational work to date and impart a sense of urgency for transformation based on a coherent vision and strategic plan for improvement.
- Convey a positive public image as a school district with great potential.

- Engage members of the district and community in mutual transformation and accountability discussions.
- Increase recruitment and hiring of a highly qualified, diverse workforce.
- Serve as the district's most vocal promoter and supporter.

The basic rationale was to present ideas of a draft plan I had given the board in my job interview and then provide it in meetings as a starting point with key leaders and stakeholders. Over the ninety days, our intent was to revise the proposed plan based on feedback from the listening tour. As a result, we would develop a coherent vision, mission, values, goals, and objectives that addressed the district's current challenges and ensure a sense of urgency and focus on student achievement.

As part of an internal transformation, it is critical to review and adjust, as needed, the

- governance model;
- roles of the board and superintendent;
- process and procedures for board meetings, workshops, committees, and administrative support;
- policy development and oversight; and
- civic involvement and capacity in transitional planning.

The overall goals presented to the community for consideration in the listening tour needed to be:

- Increase student achievement.
- Ensure effective district governance through positive board/superintendent relations.
- Improve public trust and confidence through open, honest communication and positive relationships.
- Increase organizational effectiveness and efficiency.
- Establish a supportive, positive district climate and culture.

At the end of the ninety-day listening tour, the deliverable needs to be a strategic plan for approval by the board of education.

KEY INSIGHTS FROM CHAPTER TWO
Embrace complexity.

- Educational transformation mirrors complex systems— like the *Columbia* space shuttle—where failure is rarely due to a single factor. Similarly, solutions in education must be multifaceted and deeply integrated.
- Success requires not isolated fixes or a hodgepodge of initiatives but a cohesive, systemic strategy built on a complex, responsive design.

Ownership is critical.

- Ownership equals motivation.
- Every stakeholder—students, teachers, parents, community—must be encouraged to own the vision and reimagine what schools can be.

- Leadership must distribute responsibility and create synergy through inclusivity and responsiveness to the community's specific context.

Lead by inspiration rather than by command.

- Effective leadership is about inspiring people to move together, not racing ahead alone.
- As Bruce Buchanan wrote, the superintendent role is "part education expert, part CEO, and part tent revival preacher."

Set the stage for transformation.

- A new superintendent must immediately make people believe change is possible and inspire them to commit to a strategic direction.
- Begin by ensuring that all stakeholders—board, staff, students, parents, and community partners—see themselves as part of the solution.

A listening tour can be a strategic accelerator.

- Traditional ninety-day listening tours are often followed by slow strategic planning. Given APS's urgent needs, a parallel process of listening and co-creating a plan was adopted.
- A data-informed urgency drove this acceleration due to dramatic shifts in demographics, rising poverty (64 percent) and a doubling of English learners (40 percent).

Confront harsh realities.

- APS faced low achievement, poor attendance, and high dropout rates. These were symptoms of a system that had not kept pace with its community's evolving needs.
- Incrementalism was not an option—transformation, not tinkering, was required.

Focus on an integrated strategy.

- Too many districts fall for quick fixes. Real change is not about purchasing a new curriculum or reorganizing a school but rather aligning rigor, relevance, and relationships.
- Success demands a district-wide, aligned strategy, not isolated school-by-school efforts.

Establish foundational principles for systemic change.
To raise student achievement and close gaps, the district committed to:

- Build urgency around a coherent vision and strategic plan.
- Promote a positive public image and faith in public education.
- Engage the entire district and community in shared ownership and accountability.
- Recruit and hire a diverse, high-quality workforce.
- Be the district's loudest advocate and champion.

Review and adjust critical aspects of internal transformation.

Critical areas reviewed and adjusted as part of internal transformation included:

- Governance and board/superintendent roles
- Meeting structures and policy development
- Civic engagement in planning

Outcomes of the listening tour.

The ultimate deliverable from the tour was a strategic plan for board approval with:

- Community input and ownership
- Increased student achievement and close the achievement gap
- Effective governance through healthy board/superintendent relations
- Improved public trust via honest communication
- Organizational efficiency
- Positive district climate and culture

CHAPTER QUESTIONS TO CONSIDER

1. **Reflecting on Leadership:** How do you think the leadership principles discussed here could apply to your own organization or community? What changes might you make based on these ideas?
2. **Complex Systems in Education:** What are some complex challenges within your school district

or organization that might require a multifaceted approach to solve? How can you start addressing them?

3. **Strategic Planning:** If you were to create a strategic plan for your organization, what key elements would you include to ensure it is not just a collection of initiatives but a cohesive strategy?

4. **Listening to Stakeholders:** How important do you think it is to engage stakeholders early in the process of transformation? What are some ways you can start a listening tour in your context?

5. **Transformational Change:** What do you believe are the biggest barriers to achieving transformational change in education or your current field? How can you overcome them?

6. **Building Capacity for Leadership:** How can you foster leadership at all levels within your organization? What steps can you take to empower others to take ownership of their roles?

7. **Community and Civic Engagement:** In what ways can you involve your community in the decision-making process? How can you build stronger relationships between your organization and the community it serves?

8. **Assessing Organizational Health:** What indicators would you use to assess the current health of your organization? How can you use these insights to drive improvement?

CHAPTER THREE

Owning the Case for a Transformation

I remember reading a case study that discussed the Kansas City Preventive Patrol Experiment, a groundbreaking study in the early 1970s that evaluated the effectiveness of police patrols in preventing crime. The researchers found that increasing or decreasing police presence didn't significantly affect crime rates, leading to conclusions about the importance of effective implementation in crime prevention efforts. What I learned was that even with funding and political backing, a plan can still fail. Once they developed the plan, the leadership in the city considered the problem solved and took their eyes off the implementation phase of the effort. Sure, developing a plan is never easy, but the hardest part of change is implementation. The implementation was not monitored so the grand plan failed miserably.

I subsequently came across John Kotter's book *Leading Change: Why Transformation Efforts Fail*. *Harvard Business Review* had this to say:

> *Most major change initiatives . . . generate lukewarm results. Many fail miserably. Why? Kotter maintains that too many managers don't realize transformation is a process, not an event. It advances through stages that build on each other. And, it takes years. Pressured to accelerate the process, managers skip stages. But shortcuts never work. . . . By understanding the stages of change . . . your organization flexes with tectonic shifts in competitors, markets, and technologies—leaving rivals far behind.*

Kotter describes eight stages in transformation:
1. Establish a sense of urgency.
2. Form a powerful guiding coalition.
3. Create a vision.
4. Communicate the vision.
5. Empower others to act on the vision.
6. Plan for and create short-term wins.
7. Consolidate improvements and produce more change.
8. Institutionalize new approaches.

Leading Change

Paying attention to the lessons learned in implementation from Kansas City and the guiding steps for transformation from John Kotter, we began the journey to transform Aurora Public Schools so that we would increase student achievement and close the achievement gaps—this became our litmus test in approving initiatives for our district. If an idea did not improve achievement or close the diversity gaps, we wouldn't consider it. Here are some major steps in owning an internal transformation:

Overcome bureaucratic challenges. While developing a strategic plan in the fall of 2006, I was reminded about the strong penchant for bureaucracies to resist change. In my conversations with administrators, principals, and teachers over many months, I kept hearing the phrase, "That is not the way we do it in this school district."

After hours of research, it came to my attention that APS had changed drastically in the demographic representations of the many nationalities. The school district had grown considerably and in the previous decade, as just one example, the Latino population had grown from 18 percent to over 50 percent. When I took over as superintendent, more than 120 languages were spoken in APS representing over 130 countries. This was a challenge the district hadn't fully realized nor taken on in a deliberate and planned manner during the previous decade. In my view, it was the declining student achievement and evolving demographics that required a significant sense of urgency.

Having lived or traveled in over sixty-five countries, I saw the rich value of having the incredible diversity and various cultures available for our students' learning. At the same time, the diversity required us to adjust our pedagogy to meet the needs of our changing student population. The data clearly showed that the instructional road we were on was not heading in the right direction.

So, after I was told again and again when possible solutions were suggested, "That is not the way we do things in APS," I clearly and deliberately asked what Aurora they were talking about: the school district in 1996, or the district in 2006? Was it the school district in the past where students of color were in the minority, or was it our current school district where the students of color were in the majority? With realities of poor student achievement and a changing student population, the beginnings of a sense of urgency were awakened.

Build your coalition. One of the first things we accomplished was to develop a citizens group of leaders in the district who could provide insight and recommendations on our transformational change. We formed a Superintendent's Advisory Council that comprised community leaders and organizations, including the Aurora City manager, the president of the Community College of Aurora, the president of the Chamber of Commerce, religious leaders, and representatives of various ethnic groups.

This advisory group met monthly to begin with in the first year and eventually gravitated to quarterly meetings in the second year and beyond. The advisors on the Superintendent's Advisory Council were instrumental in providing insights into initiatives in light of the local culture. However, as much an incoming superintendent can study the aspects of a new community, there is nothing that can replace the value of local leaders providing cultural understanding to standing issues. They also serve as communicators to the stakeholders in the community on what is being done and why it is being done. Their role was instrumental in evaluating the ideas that were being generated from the ninety-day listening tour and involving the community.

Although it took place after my tenure as superintendent, the Colorado Education Initiative offers another powerful example of coalition building. In 2015, six schools across three school districts were selected for grants to redesign their learning models. This effort imagined a future in which education is designed to help students develop the academic, professional, entrepreneurial, personal, and civic competencies that a modern society and economy demand. This example of coalition building was built to maximize outcomes for students and promote systems that support and incentivize educators.

Coalition building—a significant part of a successful school transformation—is discussed in more detail in the External Transformation section.

Craft your vision and mission. As a former strategic planner in the USAF, I knew that strategy is about aligning vision with action. In other words, a true strategy connects the ends—the vision—with the means—the goals and objectives needed to achieve it. At APS, what was urgently missing was exactly that: a clear, deliberate plan. We called our first strategy VISTA 2010—we selected this term because VISTA in Spanish is "View," which put our focus on the future, while the acronym stood for **V**isionary **I**nstruction **S**haping the **T**ransformation of **A**urora Public Schools. VISTA 2010 was a fifteen-page illustrated document that followed the adage, sometimes attributed to Mark Twain, that "if I had more time, I would have written you a shorter letter."

Our no-excuses, no-blame vision (END) became *Graduate every student with the choice to attend college, without remediation*. This concise statement became the hallmark of developing a sense of urgency on what was in the art of the possible. It captured a laser focus for our community to hear and understand. To "graduate every student" was meant to delineate the reason we existed for our students and it implied we should never limit a student's expectations.

We've all heard stories about the educator who told a student they were not "college material." I knew a woman who heard that just once, and its impact was so destructive that it delayed her college education by decades.

"Choice to attend college" was meant to have students understand that our job was to get them to the point of receiving a diploma fully prepared to go to a two- or four-year college or university but also to have the capability to have other choices such as the military or entering the workforce without delay. The key word was *choice*.

Finally, the direction to graduate "without remediation" was a keen focus on making sure that students were not only able to graduate but also able to start postsecondary education without having to take remedial courses before they could earn college credits. Too many of our students were arriving at colleges and universities ill prepared for the rigorous requirements of higher education and needing to start with remedial courses that added to the expense and time commitment of pursuing a degree.

The next step was to develop a mission. This part of any organization often gets confused with the vision. A vision needs to be beyond your reach at the present time. I once heard General Colin Powell, former Chairman of the Joints Chiefs of Staff and former Secretary of State, say that visions can be shared from a mountain—we may not be able to clearly define them now, but we can share the view and appreciate the direction.

There is often confusion when organizations develop strategic plans, especially regarding visions and mission statements. Visions need to be short, memorable, and able to excite and inspire passion in people to realize what is possible.

Missions, however, need to be more defined and outline what it is an organization does. The APS mission became *To teach every student within a safe environment the knowledge, skills, and values necessary to enter college or careers and become contributing members of society who flourish in a diverse, dynamic world.*

Everyone, in any organization, wants to know what the big picture is and how they can be a part of it. I totally get that. As a young Captain in the USAF, I was stationed in the Netherlands during the Cold War. In the late 1970s, we were flying combat air patrols in defense of Western Europe against the possible attack of the Warsaw Pact nations of Eastern Europe and the Soviet Union. While I knew my job, I wasn't sure at first how it fit into the overall defensive plan. Once I was briefed on how the Eastern bloc were going to come over in three waves—first Eastern European fighters to establish corridors, then the Soviet fighters to attack our command and control sites, and finally the Soviet bombers who would attack our nuclear facilities—I knew how and why I fit into the plan.

In APS, we kept our plan, the big picture, simple by dividing the goals/objectives (*means*) into four areas or "strategic pillars," as I have come to refer to them: **P**eople, **A**chievement, **C**ommunity, and **E**nvironment (PACE). This was a paradigm that everyone could understand. VISTA 2010 created a roadmap for success, but it allowed others to fill in from the bottom rather than be directed from the top. I often refer to this style as a "federalist" means to strategic planning, because anyone can bring forward ideas and develop strategies for implementing the goals. Anyone in the organization can contribute innovative and creative ideas from the bottom up, if they know the big picture. This provides the overarching umbrella for guidance but reserves the right for individual schools to propose ideas from the grassroots, similar to our federal government's relationship with the states where all rights are reserved to the states except for what the federal government reserves. This creates *ownership* and adds value to the plan.

I have used the idea of strategic pillars for different "Means" categories so everyone in the organization can tie their work to the vision. For example, I knew our plan was working when a teacher approached me one day and said she had done "People" and "Community." What she relayed to me was her initiative for "P" was helping to develop a process to select the teacher of the year in the school. She demonstrated her "C" efforts by organizing a parent assembly where the School Improvement Plan would be briefed. By having an easily understood strategic structure that everyone owns, an educational leader doesn't have to dictate every outcome; teachers and principals can fill in the gaps on their own.

However, having a plan with a vision and mission that are tied to goals and objectives isn't enough. To guard against a plan being just a grand design with no follow-through, it is important that every objective be measurable. As a leader, data can be your friend.

Through reviews of one of the four strategic pillars for PACE each month at the district leadership team level and at the board of Education, the plan can remain a living document that is continually reviewed and assessed over the course of five years.

The key goals within the strategic plan are interconnected and organized to break down the bureaucratic silos that exist in large school districts. Milestones demand accountability and visibility.

Craft your mission and vision so the emphasis is on results and identifies the district's obligation to develop an organization in which all students can learn and succeed.

Communicate the vision. There is a story about communication that I use in speeches. Communicating is like a scaffold on the side of a building. The superintendent is on the bottom, not the top. The superintendent has a bag of sand representing information, but the bag has a hole. As the bag is raised to the next level, sand or information pours out. As the bag rises up the levels in the organization, by the time it gets to the last entity, there is no sand left in the bag. This illustrates the challenge with communication.

Effective communication isn't easy. District leaders need a multitude of means of communicating with different audiences, gathering feedback from employees, students, and community members and disseminating district plans. Channels of communication include town hall meetings, surveys, social media, email, and mailed letters.

When I was a Wing Commander of a large fighter base called Luke Air Force Base, west of Phoenix, Arizona, we had a safety issue, and I needed to get the word out on corrective actions. I spent a lot of time getting the memo down to one page, adhering to the concept that if you had more time you should write a shorter letter. At the bottom of the page, I stated that the first person who read this memo and brought it to my office would get $10. The memo was posted on every bulletin board in over fifty buildings. Three weeks later, a Chief Master Sergeant who had been out of town asked me who had claimed the reward. "You have!" I replied. I learned not to depend on just one way to communicate a message and expect it to be effective.

To communicate APS's vision, we used every available means to get the word out to all our stakeholders. Communication is an art, not a science. Take the time to make sure the vision is clear, succinct, and easy to memorize.

Empower others to act. During the ninety-day listening tour, I was struck by the fact that there was tremendous variance in where teachers were at in the curriculum. We needed to align curriculum, instruction, assessment, and professional development. This responsibility needed to be delegated to the teachers, a bottom-up approach to solving a problem.

I realized that some teachers were waiting to get *all* students to an understanding of a part of the curriculum before moving on and weren't able to cover the required standards by the end of the semester. Teachers needed guidance so all the required content was covered during the semester; proficient students needed to be exposed to the full content of the curriculum, and contingency plans were needed for students requiring extra instruction. In response, pacing guides were developed by teachers and for teachers. Teachers broke material into segments with specific learning goals to ensure consistent instruction district-wide. Pacing guides are essential tools used in school districts to help standardize and streamline the delivery of curriculum across grade levels and subjects. They act as detailed road maps that outline what content should be taught and when, ensuring that all students are exposed to the same concepts at the same time, regardless of individual classroom differences. (See more on pacing guides in Chapter Five.)

Gather short wins. Administrators and teachers were coached and understood how to use data to carefully monitor student progress, identify potential problem areas, and implement student targeted intervention strategies. Horizontally integrated teams began to look at all the data, not just their own classes. By creating "data walls" (see Chapter Four for more about data walls) that displayed results for every classroom, teacher, and subject at every school, there was transparent accountability where everyone knew and understood their student proficiency levels. (This information was posted in areas where teachers worked and was not available to the public.)

This was a roundabout way of injecting a peer accountability system that was not limited by the Union Master Agreement—our comprehensive, board-approved labor contract with the teachers' union that sets compensation, benefits, workload, evaluation, and grievance processes. Most were shocked by this transparency at first but then accepted mutual responsibility for their results. This was a major cultural change with the focus on results that resulted in some quick wins on achievement.

We also introduced quarterly standards-based exams designed by our teachers. This initiative provided interim data rather than waiting for annual state exams to determine a student's progress.

By building a standards-based system, kindergarten through 12th grade, school leaders can ensure students are promoted on performance—what they knew and were able to do—instead of seat time. This subject is addressed more fully in Chapter Five.

Consolidate improvements. In the aftermath of writing VISTA 2010, the APS team was able to move to an action plan that outlined specific accountability metrics for each goal and objective in the strategic plan. But this action plan needed to be more than a document collecting dust on a shelf. Since the action plan was organized around PACE, the persons responsible for the respective objectives, timelines, and metrics used to measure success were required to report on progress monthly. It needed to be a living, breathing effort, not a static report once a year. In our case, the VISTA strategic plan and the action plan were reviewed monthly, and updates were incorporated and posted on the district website each year following board of education review and approval. Consolidate data on a monthly basis, and it can become useful and relevant to educators in being held responsible for outcomes that improve student achievement.

Institutionalize new approaches. If you are going to institutionalize change in most bureaucracies you have to pay attention to the policies of the organization. One of the more compelling tasks in the first year of transformation was to review each policy. This took more than six months. Some policies had not been reviewed or changed for decades. One of the key lessons I had learned over years in leadership roles was that policies and regulations need to reflect the organization accurately. When some norms for behavior or values aren't followed for various reasons, such as being out of date or inaccurate, people begin selectively adhering to other policies or regulations ("Why should I follow this rule when this other rule isn't being followed?"). This is the feeding ground for confusion and disorganization.

By reviewing the standing policies and regulations, we were able to remove more than eighty, change more than 100, and update the review dates for the others that stayed on the books. Institutionalizing the changes we had incorporated from the strategic plan allowed for formalizing the changes, which enhances employees' ability to read and understand the rules for an organization. This is necessary for continuity, fairness, and well-run operations.

By reviewing policies and procedures periodically, you can keep them current and avoid selective adherence by staff and students.

At APS, it wasn't just a school district that changed; it was a mindset. And mindsets, once shifted, don't go back.

KEY INSIGHTS FROM CHAPTER THREE

Implementation is the hardest part of change.

- Even the best-funded, politically supported plans can fail without disciplined implementation.
- The Kansas City policing case illustrated that lack of follow-through and monitoring can doom even the most promising initiatives.

Kotter's Eight Stages of Change provide a proven framework.

- Transformation isn't an event; it is a process.
- Leaders must avoid skipping steps and instead follow a structured progression: urgency, coalition, vision, communication, empowerment, short-term wins, consolidation, and institutionalization.
- Kotter's model became a guide for structuring the APS transformation.

Establishing a sense of urgency is critical.

- APS had undergone a dramatic demographic shift, with students of color becoming the majority.
- The data showed declining student achievement, which became the basis for establishing urgency.
- Resistance such as "that's not how we do things" had to be challenged with present-day realities.

Bureaucratic inertia must be confronted.

- Systems, especially large bureaucracies, naturally resist change.
- Changing entrenched mindsets requires both data and courageous leadership.
- Cultural shifts must accompany operational and instructional changes.

Build a strong, informed coalition.

- The Superintendent's Guidance Council brought community leaders together to support and advise the transformation.
- Involving local voices helped culturally ground decisions and initiatives and created shared ownership of outcomes.
- The Colorado Education Initiative is another example of coalition building to redesign learning with collective support.

Craft a clear, bold vision.

- Strategy is the connection of ends (vision) and means (goals/objectives).
- APS's vision was simple, ambitious, and equity-focused: *Graduate every student with the choice to attend college, without remediation.*
- A vision should be inspirational and future-oriented, reaching beyond the current capabilities.

Clarify the mission to guide daily work.

- The mission defines what the organization does every day to pursue the vision.
- APS's mission clearly focused on teaching knowledge, skills, and values to prepare students for a diverse, dynamic world.
- Vision is the "mountain view"; mission is the path to get there.

Use strategic pillars to organize the work.

- PACE (People, Achievement, Community, Environment) gave staff a simple structure to tie their work to the district's strategy.
- The federalist model empowered bottom-up innovation while keeping alignment with overarching goals.
- Educators owned the plan when they could see how their actions contributed to it.

Data-driven objectives keep the plan alive.

- Every strategic objective must be measurable and monitored.
- Regular reviews of PACE pillars kept the plan a living document and drove accountability.
- Silos were broken down by interconnecting goals and holding leaders accountable.

Communicating the vision requires strategy and creativity.

- Communication is often the most difficult part of leadership.
- To reach all stakeholders, leaders must use multi-channel approaches—from memos to town halls to social media.
- The "sand in the bag" analogy illustrates how information dilutes as it travels through layers, requiring constant reinforcement.

CHAPTER QUESTIONS TO CONSIDER

1. **Reflection on Change Management:** How do you define the difference between planning and implementation in a change initiative? Why is implementation often more challenging?

2. **Applying Kotter's Model:** How do Kotter's eight stages of transformation align with your own experiences of leading or observing change? Can you identify any stages that were skipped or inadequately addressed in your past experiences?

3. **Understanding Urgency:** In your organization, how is a sense of urgency created and communicated? What are the consequences of failing to establish this urgency?

4. **Building Coalitions:** Reflect on the importance of coalition building in your experience. Have you seen

examples where strong coalitions led to successful change, or where the lack of a coalition contributed to failure?

5. **Crafting and Communicating Vision:** How effectively does your organization communicate its vision? What strategies could improve this communication?

6. **Empowerment and Accountability:** In what ways does your organization empower individuals to act on the vision? How is accountability maintained without stifling creativity or initiative?

7. **Sustaining Change:** What strategies does your organization use to ensure that initial improvements are sustained over time? How are these improvements institutionalized?

8. **Overcoming Bureaucratic Resistance:** How does your organization address resistance to change? Can you identify any common sources of resistance within your teams or stakeholders?

CHAPTER FOUR

Earning and Owning Credibility

In any transformation, those most affected gain confidence when quick wins are evident. In an age of instant gratification, communities reasonably expect early, visible progress that builds credibility. Two focus areas to be examined next—structured literacy and truancy—serve as representative deficiencies. Identifying problems is one task; implementing solutions is another. As John Kotter's eight-step model underscores, early improvement matters to every organization. Major strategic victories are unlikely within a year; however, short, meaningful wins are both possible and necessary.

Regarding the structured literacy program that was needed in APS, we took the time and resources we had available to work this issue within the first year. By reallocating resources, using financial resources from the fund balance (sometimes referred to as the rainy day fund), and developing working teams to address the literacy challenges in the district, one approach is to:

- Identify and define the literacy challenges.
- Build on what had been developed in the district to date.
- Outline recommendations on how to fix the problem.

Three months in, we committed to a districtwide readers-writers workshop model, strengthened it with existing professional development work, and recommended organizing and training horizontal and vertical data teams for every grade. We also started to implement interim assessments that allowed us to analyze accountability. Within a year, we saw demonstrated improvement at most grade levels in reading and writing.

Regarding truancy, we put in place a "principal's pass"; 10th–12th graders could leave the school grounds for lunch if they earned a principal's pass by having a 2.75 grade point average and 93 percent attendance and were not in trouble regarding discipline issues, such as fighting or disrespect. Within one semester, we saw significant improvements in truancy, and the neighbors who lived near our high schools appreciated the drop in students hanging around their homes and streets.

During my tenure as superintendent of APS from 2006 to 2013, we implemented a proactive approach to address student truancy by personally knocking on the doors of habitually absent students. This initiative aimed to encourage students to return to school and reinforce the importance of regular attendance. Along with school board members and district truancy specialists, I conducted annual door-to-door campaigns starting in 2006. These visits allowed for direct, one-on-one interactions with students and their families, providing support and resources to help them return to the classroom. As a result of these efforts, the district saw a decrease in habitual truancy rates by over 30 percent in the first two years.

Beyond these campaigns, I emphasized the critical role of daily attendance, often stating, "Every single day is important. When they disrupt their instruction, it really puts them behind." My commitment to reducing truancy was part of a broader strategy that led to improvements in student proficiency rates and graduation rates, and a reduction in dropout rates during my tenure.

These door-knocking campaigns not only addressed truancy but also strengthened the relationship between APS and the community, demonstrating our district's dedication to student success. The initiative gained significant media attention across Colorado, with local news outlets covering our efforts to re-engage students. Newspapers, television stations, and radio programs highlighted our approach, bringing awareness to the importance of school attendance and the district's commitment to supporting students and families. This publicity helped amplify the message that every student's presence in the classroom matters, further reinforcing the community's role in ensuring student success. This hands-on approach served as a model for other districts facing similar challenges, showing that leadership engagement at all levels can drive meaningful change in public education.

Additionally, the first year and every year after at the beginning of the school year, I made it a priority to ride the school bus with students. More than just a symbolic gesture, this was an opportunity to experience firsthand what thousands of students encountered daily. By riding the bus, I could assess the transportation system's efficiency, safety, and overall student experience.

These rides gave me direct insight into the challenges students faced before even stepping into the classroom. I observed everything from long ride times and logistical concerns to the social dynamics among students. Talking with students and bus drivers during these rides helped build relationships and allowed me to hear their concerns and suggestions. For many students, seeing the superintendent on their bus sent a powerful message—I cared about their journey, both literally and figuratively.

The impact of this initiative extended beyond the bus ride itself; it reinforced a culture of engagement and accessibility within the district. It signaled to staff, students, and parents that leadership wasn't confined to an office but was actively present in the daily realities of school life. Drivers appreciated the recognition of their critical role in student success, and school leaders gained a better understanding of how transportation influenced attendance, punctuality, and readiness to learn.

Riding the school bus each year was a simple but meaningful way to connect with students and ensure that decisions about transportation and school logistics were grounded in real experiences, not just reports and data.

Develop an Integrated Mosaic of Integrated Initiatives

One of the common failures I have seen in working an organizational transformation is the tendency for initiative disintegration. When there is a hodgepodge of initiatives that are not integrated toward a common goal, the result is almost always failure.

When discussing our work of APS, I often quote NASA Apollo 13 Mission Director Gene Krantz, who said, "Failure is not an option and hope is not a strategy." Parents not only entrust us with their children, they also assume that we are doing everything possible to ensure their children's success. It is our moral imperative to meet these expectations and not fail our students, and our efforts have to be integrated. While hope is important to instill in our students and families, it is not a strategy that maximizes efficiency and effectiveness.

We have the professional duty as educators to create and execute strategies that would build on district realities and actionable initiatives that are tied together to accelerate student achievement and close the achievement gaps.

The *how* of improving achievement often frustrates school district leaders. To circumvent this, we established the strategic plan discussed in Chapter Three to encompass our initiatives so ends (vision) were connected to means (goals and objectives). Launching multiple initiatives that were fully aligned and integrated maximized our chances to be successful for our students.

Coming from a military background and business experience, I was surprised at the extent silos persisted in public education and how little communication there was between staff in classrooms, schools, and district offices. We began by communicating the overarching vision to serve all our students successfully so they would have the choice to attend a college or university of their choosing. As stated previously, our mission became our ability "to teach every student in a safe environment the knowledge, skills and values necessary to enter college or a career and become a contributing member of society who flourishes in a diverse, dynamic world."

The aim was unequivocal—*every student*—with no excuses and no blame, a hallmark motto that would eventually embody our formal strategic plan. From this, we began to structure a cohesive set of goals and objectives with which to innovate and transform the district.

Five main priorities can guide the development of an integrated strategic plan:

- Increase student achievement.

- Ensure effective district governance through positive superintendent/board relations.
- Improve public trust and confidence through open communications and positive relationships.
- Increase organizational effectiveness and efficiency.
- Establish a supportive and positive district culture.

Each goal in VISTA 2010 included an integrated set of activities and measurable results that explicitly identify what is needed to meet the objective.

As mentioned in Chapter Three, we organized our goals around four key strategic pillars—People, Achievement, Community, and Environment (PACE)—that represented our focus. PACE was intended to be a concept for stakeholders to easily understand and hopefully support. The graphic in the figure below shows a sample of the mosaic of initiatives that form the basis for the approach. If people

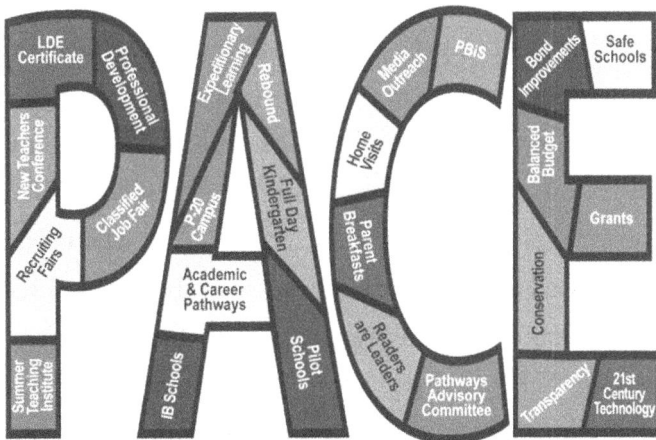

Listings of Major Initiatives for PACE

understand the integration and big picture, the strategic plan has a higher likelihood of succeeding.

Harness the Power of "Noticing and Naming"

In Peter Johnston's book *Choice Words,* he discusses "noticing and naming." In APS we built on this phrase to describe the necessity to "notice" challenges and "name" solutions. For instance, if there is courageous feedback that a part of the strategic mosaic is not working, then the work must come full circle. When this communication is made, it is absolutely requires that leadership acknowledge the issue. However, even when there is a strong effort to resolve the issue, there can be a significant problem regarding implementation. The challenge is that the resolution is rarely communicated to the originator and may not be recognized by the person who submitted the input.

How can that happen? It is not uncommon for a remedy to be limited sometimes by funding, policy, law, or timing. If leadership doesn't get back to the person who submitted the problem, they may not realize it was even resolved or addressed. Supervisors need to close that loop, explaining what was or was not done based on the identified challenge.

For example, we had a principal meeting where inputs were requested for possible budget cuts in light of the recession in 2008. Submissions were collected, district leadership incorporated many of the ideas in deliberations with the board of education, and decisions were made. The problem was we never got back to the principals on how we integrated their inputs into the discussions and what changes were made based on their contributions. We "noticed" the inputs but never "named' the solutions arrived at by district governance. If you didn't have all the information, you couldn't recognize the varied efforts to integrate the inputs into the budget. This is a key implementation process that needs to be matured and owned by leadership.

Dig Down to Root Causes and Expectations

In Colorado there is an accountability requirement for every school to develop a Unified Improvement Plan (UIP). APS had an internal requirement for a School Improvement Plan for years, so I wasn't excited that we had a state-driven requirement to develop yet another way of determining a plan. However, there was a key element to the UIP that was new for APS—the specificity to study root causes for any deficiencies in student achievement. This has become a very valuable tool for school districts.

Simply put, a root cause analysis delves down into asking "why" there is a problem. As a young child is prone to do with a parent in asking why, why, why, until he or she gives up or the parent is finally able to resolve the question, this process has proved effective for adults in schools. By asking the why question repeatedly, a school is able to get to the basic cause of poor student achievement or the reason why achievement gaps are occurring.

Here's another thing that surprised me. Inevitably, in every school, there was a root cause identified that centered around expectations. Some schools had real problems with expectations for their students, and the blame game included that they were too poor, they did not speak English, or they came from disruptive families. As I discovered, there was a need for equity training so teachers and administrators could more fully understand how race can play into our expectations.

To be clear, I rarely encountered a teacher or administrator who lacked genuine care for students. The challenge was that their compassion was not always balanced with clear expectations. In their desire to support struggling students, they sometimes accepted lower standards or offered excuses for why those students were not succeeding.

Let me demonstrate this with a story. One day I was visiting a school and I witnessed a white, female teacher talking to a young African American student. It was very clear to me that this student adored this teacher and the teacher clearly had a strong affection for this child. When they finished talking, I went over to the teacher and told her how impressed I was with the relationship she had with the student and that there clearly was a strong bond between the two of them. I then asked her how the young man was doing and she said, "Amazing!" I thought, what more could I ask for? There was a relationship and there was achievement. But then I asked for data about the student's academic standing. And he was *not* doing amazing. He was doing terribly, especially since we had him since kindergarten and now he was a third grader. What I realized was this teacher was telling me that was the best he could do—he was doing "amazing." The heart was there, but the head did not hold the expectation that every child can learn. We can "love" our students to failure if we don't hold high expectations for every child.

Believing that every child can learn must not be a slogan or platitude. It truly must be believed if we are going to close the diversity achievement gaps.

Pick a Fight You Can Win: Managed Instruction vs. Autonomy

While developing credibility in proving the new transformation was beneficial to the school district, it was important to pick a problem that all could relate to, one that definitely needed fixing, and one I had confidence that we could fix.

One of the key debates I discovered in my first few months while attending the Broad Superintendents Academy was the differences between managed instruction and autonomy. For example, *managed instruction* is a top-down strategy in developing a district-wide common curriculum with strong district control over budgets and centralized control overall. *Autonomy* is allowing for more freedom on curriculum and budget at the school level but with high accountability. An example of managed instruction is the Aldine Independent School District in Texas, the winner of the 2009 Broad Prize for Urban Education. This district has a comprehensive, fully integrated, and aligned curriculum and instructional system that sets clear, rigorous expectations for teachers and principals and provides ready access to instructional resources and student achievement information. According to the Broad Prize selection methodology, Aldine outperformed other districts in Texas that serve students with similar socioeconomic conditions in reading and math at all school levels.

One example of autonomy is the STRIVE Preparatory schools, a charter school system in Colorado. It is a Denver-based network of free, open enrollment, public charter schools committed to providing every student with an excellent, rigorous, college-preparatory education. In 2011, STRIVE Prep's schools ranked as four of the top five secondary schools in Denver Public Schools, all earning the district's highest rating of "Distinguished." Among the 137 schools evaluated, the schools ranked in the top 11.

In working to get some quick wins in 2006–2007, it was important to understand what was working and what was not working in APS and to adopt a management structure that district personnel could understand and own. In 2006, the debate over managed instruction and autonomy was in its infancy. In APS we debated the various models that would fit the culture in our district. It was clear, however, that the district needed some structures to foster momentum.

While touring the district in the first ninety days, I learned that there was no unified approach to literacy in the district. When I asked for the literacy curriculum, I was handed a five-page continuum. While I was visiting schools and talking with stakeholders, the feedback continually came back to the fact that there were varied approaches to reading and writing and there was a need for structure. Even the Aurora Education Association (Teacher's Union) discussed the need for more rigor in our literacy program.

There was a strong desire to have a more structured approach since the variants of instruction were confusing for veteran teachers and especially so for new teachers. Complicating the matter, students from different elementary schools fed into middle school or high school with various instructional foundations for literacy. This became obvious when I asked every school to have students write a prompt on their summer experience and every principal was to bring an example of proficient work at every grade level. The levels of evidence of proficiency varied, which demonstrated that we did not have a clear understanding of what proficiency looked like in the various grade levels. As a starting point, we needed to provide a more managed and centralized approach to our writing.

Another key area of concern, as previously addressed, was truancy in the district. When I visited some of our secondary schools, especially high school, there were so many students walking around the neighborhood that I wasn't sure whether school was in or out! Complaints from neighborhoods around our high schools were increasing, and there was a clear frustration from our community regarding students trespassing and being loud.

While I served as a board member and Executive Director for the *Columbia* Accident Investigation Board in 2003, the investigation team enlisted the services of Diane Vaughn, author of *The Challenger Launch Decision: Risky Technology, Culture, and Deviance at NASA*. In her book she described "normalizing deviance" where actions and effects get viewed as non-deviant or, what some people might describe as a "normal cost of doing business." Truancy in APS had reached a level where it became a norm in that the cost and challenge of dealing with truancy was so prohibitive it became accepted as "normal."

In 2003 while investigating the *Columbia* shuttle mishap, I became a serious student of culture. We defined organizational culture as follows:

> *Organizational culture refers to the basic values, norms, beliefs, and practices that characterize the functioning of a particular institution. At the most basic level, organizational culture defines the assumptions that employees make as they carry out their work; it defines "the way we do things here." An organization's culture is a powerful force that persists through reorganizations and the departure of key personnel.*

It became obvious to me as the new superintendent that the culture in APS had normalized the deviant reality of truancy. Our habitual truancy rate was defined as a student who had missed four unexcused classes in any month or 10 unexcused classes in any year, and our truancy was approaching 30 percent.

Using the evidence gathered around the lack of a literacy structure and increasing truancy—two areas I knew could be fixed—it was our decision to move to a more managed instruction model for APS.

The ninety-day listening tour had uncovered other areas where centralized control would enable a more focused and comprehensive paradigm for instructional transformation, such as:

- A lack of instructional pacing guides to ensure content was covered in each subject area
- Little evidence of accountability data
- Lack of data-based decision-making
- Lack of teamwork within and between schools
- Lack of strategic leadership training for principals
- Lack of equity training in a school district where over 70 percent of the students were students of color and the student body spoke more than one hundred languages

I need to make this clear: I am not an advocate for managed instruction as the sole means of transforming a school district. In fact, it is my opinion that managed instruction can only get a district to a certain level of student achievement and then it will stagnate around the 50 percent level. However, I have concluded it is best to start with managed instruction in low-performing K-12 institutions until a school has demonstrated the organizational prowess and leadership to graduate to the more challenging model of autonomy. This does not presuppose a "new" school that is built from the ground up could not start with autonomy. However, a school that is not accelerating student achievement and closing achievement gaps should demonstrate the proper leadership, pedagogy, and high expectations before moving to autonomous instruction. APS learned this the hard way when we adopted models of autonomy such as Boston's Pilot School Concept (launched in 1994 to create models of educational innovation) and Innovation schools that were approved for use in Colorado in 2010. If a school moves to these paradigms without solid leadership and a culture of proven accountability, their chances of success are clearly limited. Any organization must earn and *own* its credibility.

KEY INSIGHTS FROM CHAPTER FOUR
Early wins build credibility.

- Quick wins matter: In a transformation, early measurable improvements (e.g., in literacy and truancy) help generate credibility, motivation, and belief that change is possible.
- Structured literacy gains: APS achieved measurable literacy improvement within one year by reallocating resources, establishing curriculum frameworks, and initiating interim assessments.
- Truancy interventions worked: Simple but effective programs like the "principal's pass" and door-to-door

truancy campaigns yielded tangible attendance gains and strengthened community ties.

Leadership visibility increases trust.

- Leading by example: Riding school buses with students reinforced the superintendent's accessibility, highlighted unseen operational issues, and strengthened student and staff relationships.
- Engagement signals care: Leadership presence in students' day-to-day experiences helped create a culture of commitment and visibility.

Integration prevents initiative failure.

- **Avoid the "initiative soup":** Disconnected or overlapping programs—each with its own goals, timelines, and champions—can overwhelm staff and confuse stakeholders. For example, if a district launches separate initiatives for literacy, attendance, and social-emotional learning without coordination, schools may struggle to implement them all effectively. Transformation requires aligned, integrated efforts with a shared purpose and mutually reinforcing goals.
- **PACE framework:** The People, Achievement, Community, and Environment (PACE) strategic pillars helped APS communicate its priorities in a unified, strategic format. Each goal/objective/initiative was mapped to one or more of these four pillars, which provided

coherence and made it easier for staff and community members to see how the pieces fit together.

- **Mosaic of initiatives:** Unlike "initiative soup," a mosaic presents different efforts as parts of a bigger picture. For instance, when APS aligned its early literacy initiative (Achievement) with a parent engagement campaign (Community) and professional development for teachers (People), stakeholders could see how each contributed to improving student outcomes. When initiatives are visibly interrelated and tied to a common vision—like the four PACE priorities—buy-in increases because everyone sees their role in the larger transformation.

For authentic communication, notice issues and name solutions.

- Feedback loops are essential: Listening to input isn't enough—leaders must *notice* issues and *name* the actions taken in response.
- Transparency builds trust: Closing the communication loop (e.g., explaining budget decisions influenced by principal input) avoids alienation and builds shared ownership.

Root cause analysis reveals hidden barriers.

- Digging deeper: Unified Improvement Plans taught APS to look beyond surface problems and interrogate underlying causes.

- Low expectations as a root cause to barriers: In many schools, gaps in achievement were linked to low expectations masked by strong personal relationships.
- Equity lens needed: Teachers should care about their students—but love without high expectations can lead to failure. Equity training helped staff connect head and heart.

Create a culture of high expectations.

- Every child can learn: This belief must be internalized, not just stated. High expectations, when combined with support, are crucial to student success.
- Data vs. perception: Strong relationships must be matched with honest academic assessment to avoid reinforcing low performance with emotional rationalizations.

For strategic focus, pick a fight you can win.

- Managed instruction vs. autonomy: APS focused on centralized strategies (e.g., common curriculum, data teams) where results could be driven quickly and systemically.
- Select visible, solvable issues: Choosing winnable challenges builds momentum and demonstrates the competence of leadership.

CHAPTER QUESTIONS TO CONSIDER

1. **Reflecting on Your Experience:** In your own work or personal experiences, have you ever witnessed the impact of achieving quick wins? How did those early successes influence the overall success of the project or initiative?

2. **Identifying Quick Wins:** In your current organization or community, what are some areas where you could identify and pursue quick wins? How would you prioritize them?

3. **Managing Expectations:** How do you balance the need to show early results with the long-term goals of a transformation? What strategies can you use to ensure that early wins don't compromise the overall vision?

4. **Initiative Integration:** Have you encountered situations where multiple initiatives were not well integrated? How did this affect the outcome? What steps could you take to ensure that different initiatives work together toward a common goal?

5. **Cultural Change:** How does the concept of "noticing and naming" apply to the culture within your organization? What challenges have you faced in implementing feedback and ensuring that it is communicated effectively?

6. **Root Cause Analysis:** What methods do you use to identify the root causes of challenges in your work?

How do these methods help you avoid quick fixes and instead focus on sustainable solutions?

7. **Managed Instruction vs. Autonomy:** Which approach do you believe would be more effective in your organization—managed instruction or autonomy? Why? How would you implement or balance these approaches?

8. **Equity and Expectations:** How do you ensure that high expectations are maintained for all students, regardless of their background? What steps can be taken to prevent "loving students to failure"?

CHAPTER FIVE

Owning and Orchestrating a Transformation

Transformations are not easy, and people typically don't like change. Therefore, it is imperative to equip leadership with data that supports the need for change. In the case of Aurora Public Schools (APS), data showed that achievement in literacy and math had been dropping for the past three years. The data clearly showed we needed to turn the district around and accelerate student achievement. The challenge was developing a momentum for urgency.

As I have learned, you cannot turn the entire "ship" around in one year. But you can gain some champions, in this case, proactive principals who had the courage and leadership prowess to lead the way. The idea is to find leaders in the organization who have the skill sets needed to try transformative ideas *and* who have the respect of their peers.

When these leaders show results, the naysayers start to fall in line.

As we worked through our plan, VISTA 2010, we worked a transformation that I argued rivaled anything in the country. While that is a bold statement, I could back it up with the following detailed list that captures about half of what was changed through innovation.

New Literacy Programs K-12

APS implemented several new K-12 literacy programs aimed at improving student reading proficiency, particularly in response to district-wide achievement gaps and the need for early intervention. These initiatives were part of APS's broader commitment to improving literacy outcomes, ensuring that students developed strong reading skills early and continued to grow as proficient readers throughout their education.

Literacy Interventions for Early Grades

- **CORE Reading Program:** APS introduced a district-wide, research-based literacy framework to support K-3 students. This program emphasized phonemic awareness, phonics, fluency, vocabulary, and comprehension.
- **Full-Day Kindergarten Expansion:** Recognizing the importance of early literacy development, APS expanded access to full-day kindergarten, allowing more instructional time focused on reading readiness.

- **Dynamic Indicators of Basic Early Literacy Skills (DIBELS) and Progress Monitoring:** APS implemented DIBELS assessments to track reading proficiency in the early grades and provide targeted interventions for struggling readers.

Secondary Literacy Initiatives

- **Read 180:** APS expanded the use of Read 180, a blended learning program designed to support struggling readers in upper elementary, middle, and high school through adaptive instruction and personalized learning pathways.
- **Literacy Across Content Areas:** To improve reading comprehension beyond English classes, APS integrated literacy instruction into science, social studies, and math curricula, ensuring that students practiced reading strategies in all subjects.
- **Professional Development for Teachers:** The district provided ongoing training for teachers in evidence-based literacy instruction, including strategies for differentiating reading instruction to meet diverse student needs.

Parent and Community Engagement

- **Family Literacy Nights:** Schools hosted literacy events where parents learned strategies to support reading at home, reinforcing the connection between school and home literacy practices.

- **Partnerships with Libraries and Community Organizations:** APS worked with local libraries and non-profits to provide students with greater access to books and literacy resources outside of school hours.

English Language Learner (ELL) Literacy Support

- **Sheltered Instruction Observation Protocol (SIOP):** To better support the district's growing ELL population, APS implemented SIOP strategies to integrate language development with content learning.
- **Dual Language and Biliteracy Programs:** APS expanded bilingual education options to support native Spanish speakers in developing literacy in both English and Spanish.

Pacing Guides

Between 2006 and 2013, APS implemented pacing guides as curriculum planning tools to promote consistency and alignment with state standards across the district. These guides were not intended as rigid, day-to-day lesson plans, but as road maps outlining the sequence and timing of essential content. Their purpose was to help teachers balance depth with coverage—ensuring that instruction did not linger too long on a single topic and risk leaving other parts of the curriculum untouched, even for proficient students. By providing a clear framework for what needed to be taught over a period of time, pacing guides supported teachers in organizing instruction, monitoring student progress, and reinforcing APS's commitment to data-driven improvement.

Standards-Based Alignment

- The pacing guides were aligned with Colorado Academic Standards and later adapted to incorporate elements of the Common Core State Standards as they were introduced.
- They outlined essential skills and knowledge that students needed to master at each grade level, ensuring alignment across classrooms and schools.

Structured Scope and Sequence

- The guides provided a week-by-week breakdown of instructional content across core subjects such as literacy, math, science, and social studies.
- They ensured that key concepts were introduced at appropriate times and reinforced throughout the year, preventing gaps in instruction.

Formative and Summative Assessment Integration

- APS incorporated benchmark assessments at regular intervals to measure student progress and identify areas where additional support was needed.
- The pacing guides included suggested formative assessments (e.g., quizzes, exit tickets, classroom discussions)

and summative assessments (e.g., unit tests, district-wide interim assessments).

Differentiation and Intervention Strategies

- Recognizing the diverse needs of APS students, the guides included modifications and scaffolding strategies for ELLs, special education students, and those performing above or below grade level.
- The guides referenced intervention programs such as Read 180 and DIBELS monitoring to support struggling readers.

Literacy and Math Focus

- Literacy pacing guides emphasized phonemic awareness, guided reading, comprehension strategies, and writing development across K-12.
- Math pacing guides ensured alignment with the Everyday Mathematics curriculum (used in elementary schools) and later transitioned to Common Core-aligned math instruction in middle and high schools.

Flexibility and Teacher Autonomy

- While the pacing guides provided a structured framework, APS encouraged teacher collaboration and Professional Learning Communities to adapt instruction based on student needs.

- Some flexibility was built in for re-teaching concepts and addressing student misconceptions before moving on to new material.

Impact on APS Instruction

- **Consistency:** Ensured that all students received a coherent and equitable curriculum, regardless of their school or teacher.
- **Accountability:** Provided a clear roadmap for administrators and instructional coaches to support teachers and track student progress.
- **Student Outcomes:** Helped drive literacy and math improvements by structuring interventions and targeted instructional time.

Data Walls

APS implemented data walls as a critical tool for tracking student progress, informing instruction, and driving school improvement. These visual displays of student performance data were used in schools across the district to promote data-driven decision-making and collaborative problem-solving among teachers and administrators. APS's use of data walls was instrumental in fostering a culture of continuous improvement and data-driven instruction, helping drive progress in key academic areas across the district.

Tracking Student Progress in Real Time

* Data walls visually represented student performance trends using color-coded charts, graphs, and student groupings.
* Data walls primarily focused on literacy and math performance, tracking progress on assessments such as DIBELS, Colorado Student Assessment Program (CSAP) and later Transitional Colorado Assessment Program (TCAP), district benchmark assessments, and formative classroom assessments.

Identifying At-Risk Students and Intervention Needs

* Students were categorized into performance tiers (e.g., at risk, approaching proficiency, proficient, advanced) to help teachers quickly identify who needed additional support.
* APS targeted interventions such as Read 180, Success-Maker, and small-group instruction based on the data.

Letting Data Drive Instruction

* Teachers and school leaders used data walls to adjust lesson plans, differentiate instruction, and set academic goals based on real-time student performance.
* Schools held weekly or bi-weekly data meetings where teams of teachers analyzed the data wall and discussed student growth patterns.

Encouraging Teacher Collaboration

- Professional Learning Communities used data walls to share instructional strategies and align teaching practices.
- Principals and instructional coaches facilitated data conversations to ensure teachers used assessments effectively.

Increasing Accountability and Transparency

- School leaders, teachers, and district administrators could monitor progress at the classroom, grade, and school levels.
- Data walls helped drive performance-based discussions, ensuring that interventions were working and holding educators accountable for student growth.

Connecting with Students and Families

- Some schools used student-friendly data walls where students tracked their own progress, setting personal academic goals and taking ownership of their learning.
- Parent-teacher conferences included discussions on data wall trends to communicate student progress and needs.

Impact on APS Schools

- More targeted and timely interventions for struggling students.

- Improved teacher collaboration and data analysis skills.
- Greater accountability at all levels—teachers, students, and administrators.
- Shift from "teaching to the test" to "teaching to student needs" by using ongoing assessment data.

Interim Assessments Devised by Teachers
Frequent, Standards-Aligned Checkpoints

- APS administered interim assessments every 6–9 weeks to measure student progress on state standards that were uniformly applied across all schools by grade level.
- These tests covered core subjects such as literacy and math and were aligned to the district's pacing guides to ensure consistency across schools.

Data-Driven Instructional Adjustments

- Unlike end-of-year tests that provided results only after students had moved on, interim assessments allowed teachers to adjust instruction in real time.
- Teachers used item-level analysis to identify strengths and weaknesses, targeting instruction where students struggled the most.

Identifying and Supporting At-Risk Students

- Schools used assessment results to identify students who were falling behind early in the year, rather than waiting for year-end scores.

- Targeted interventions were deployed using flexible grouping, small-group instruction, and additional resources such as Read 180 and SuccessMaker.

Professional Learning Communities and Data Meetings

Teachers met in Professional Learning Communities and data team meetings after each assessment cycle to review student performance trends, adjust lesson plans based on student needs, and share best practices and interventions.

Increasing Teacher and School Accountability

- Interim assessment data was used in teacher evaluations and school improvement planning.
- Principals and district leaders monitored assessment trends to provide targeted support to struggling schools and teachers.
- Interim assessment results were captured on data walls.

Preparing Students for State Assessments

- These assessments provided students with regular exposure to the testing format, reducing test anxiety and improving performance on CSAP/TCAP.
- Data from interim assessments helped APS predict end-of-year performance and take corrective actions before it was too late.

5th Block Summer Program

APS's 5th Block was unique because it focused on students with academic potential rather than those already failing, reinforcing the district's commitment to accelerating growth instead of just remediating failure.

Targeted Student Selection for Summer Program

- Students were identified through interim assessment results, classroom performance, and teacher recommendations.
- Students were invited based on specific academic criteria, including demonstrated growth during the school year; performing just below proficiency but showing potential for further progress; and regular attendance and engagement during the regular school year.

Extended Learning Time Without Starting Over

- The program lasted five weeks (hence "5th Block"), typically running from late May to June.
- Students continued learning with the same pacing guides and curriculum frameworks from the school year, instead of starting over or reviewing outdated material.

Core Focus Areas: Literacy and Math

- Instruction emphasized reading, writing, and math skills, helping students strengthen skills needed for success in the next grade.

- Teachers used small-group instruction, hands-on activities, and technology-based learning tools.

High-Quality Teaching Staff

- APS selected strong teachers with a record of effective instruction and student growth.
- Teachers used data-driven instruction to tailor lessons to students' specific needs.

Avoiding "Summer Slide"

- Research indicated that many students, especially from low-income backgrounds, lost academic progress over the summer.
- 5th Block provided continuous learning to help students retain and build upon their progress.

Impact of 5th Block in APS

- **Improved student proficiency:** Many participating students started the next school year at or near grade level, closing learning gaps.
- **Higher student engagement:** Students responded positively to smaller class sizes, hands-on learning, and the structured environment.
- **Stronger teacher-student relationships:** Continuity with effective teachers helped reinforce learning and build confidence.

- **Reduced learning loss:** The program mitigated summer learning loss, especially for students at risk of falling behind.

While these initiatives were under our PACE strategic pillars, we were not able to institute all these changes in every school right away. However, *by recruiting reform-courageous principals who could champion various parts of the transformation list*, we were able to attain valuable data on what was working and what was not and have these champions, who had credibility in the district, promote the initiatives with other school leaders as they evolved.

By assembling volunteer leaders who are courageous and skilled at seeing possibilities of improvement, you can develop a cadre of spokespersons who can communicate the value of an initiative to their peers rather than have the initiative dictated from the top. These spokespersons must be insightful enough to see the full potential of an initiative and courageous enough to point out where improvement is needed.

Once a new idea has been tried and tested, there should be ample evidence to measure whether it is worth pursuing. However, if there are still concerns, there is great merit and credibility in listing it as unsatisfactory and moving on.

There is a caution, however. While some contrarians will bring up the need for more data before a decision is made, there must be a willingness to make a decision without 100 percent assurance of success or years of data to back up a decision. There will never be enough money or time to get 100 percent of the information or data to make a foolproof decision. I have often said in my varied careers that if I could have 60 percent of the information needed to make a decision, I would be overjoyed. Remember the old saying: "The enemy of good is better."

Allocate Funding for Transformational Initiatives

A key challenge of any school district centers around funding for a transformation. I have been asked many times how we were able to pay for the initiatives in our strategic plan.

Here is another surprise that I realized. First, I have never been in any organization in the public sector that did not have areas that could be cut and be more efficient. Oftentimes, bureaucracies cannot see the "rock in the road" that is obvious to a newcomer in the organization. In 2006, it was apparent to me that the school district could absorb a 2 percent cut, across the board, in staff functions. I can remember a board member telling me that in the twenty-plus years he and his wife had been on the board of education, this had never been done. The 2 percent cut was made with very minimal impact on the classroom and minor impacts on staff functions at the district level. And it provided the stimulus money to start working the strategic plan.

Another way to allocate resources is reprioritizing programs. This is often a more painful process where staff functions must effectively do "zero-based" budgeting in justifying every budget line item. While this is very labor-intensive, it can be worked judiciously.

In Boston, an organization called the District Management Group (DMG) partners with public school district leaders to improve student outcomes, operational efficiency, and resource allocation. They do an excellent job in diving deep on issues for school districts, particularly around resource allocation.

When APS was first hit with the recession of 2008, we worked with DMG to develop a process to prioritize. Their efforts helped redesign and support budgets to better reflect the priorities of the district aligned with increasing student achievement by:

- Identifying priorities
- Understanding the context with data collection and interviews
- Analyzing and evaluating current programs—what is working and what is not

We developed a budget advisory committee made up of all representative employee groups, Chamber of Commerce leaders, district bankers, parent advisory council members, and city council officials. Their advice and counsel were helpful in establishing ideas and communicating evolving strategies on how to work the budget and still make progress on our strategic initiatives.

Employee and community surveys were also valuable in getting feedback on additional approaches or reprioritizing the draft focus areas. Surveys also served as a way to keep the community at large informed of our efforts.

When and How Far to Push Your Organization

As a leader, it is important to understand your organization's capacity to absorb change. I realized early on there was tremendous capacity in APS but we were not taking full advantage of all the talent that was available. One never knows how far to push an organization when you begin a transformation, but the analogy I use refers to a 10-pound container.

Assume for a moment that every organization has a capacity for change that can fit into a 10-pound container, but the members of the organization are only up to 6 pounds of capacity. As you move on transformational initiatives, you need to mind the limits that can be accepted. Sooner or later, you will reach full capacity (full 10-pound bag) of the acceptance of changes—but you cannot stop there. There will always be new initiatives you will need to work on or implement because of state or federal government dictate.

What happens when the bag is already full—when you can't expect people to work beyond a reasonable limit without risking burnout, illness, or even losing them from the organization?

The demonstration of a well-led organization that has reached its capacity for change is when you have leaders prioritize or push back on what can be done. A strong organization, however, needs a safe environment in which leaders, especially the superintendent, can accept criticism. However, there is a responsibility for subordinates to come to the table with solutions. Subordinates must be empowered to adjust the 10 pounds by coming up with ideas on how to adjust, change, or just stop doing some tasks.

Sometimes you will need to delay a program to fit into the capacity limits. Other times, you may need to stop doing something. The 10-pound container can adjust what is inside to allow for additional challenges. But there still is an underlying responsibility for subordinates to be part of the solution; this breeds trust and teamwork.

Here is a key insight I have gained over many years. Employees at all levels must:

- Define the problem. Since employees are bringing it to the attention of a leader, they have a vested interest in defining the problem in a clear and succinct manner. Often the effects of problems are discussed and not the true problem. Is it a problem of training? Or budget? Or personalities?
- Explain how they are working to fix the problem within their allowable resources. They have to have demonstrated they have tried to work the problem with the resources and authority they have been given.
- Suggest a few practical options that could help resolve the issue or improve the situation. These options should be specific and actionable, giving the leader a clearer path for decision-making. For example, the

employee might recommend delaying a deadline, reassigning a task, reducing the scope of work, or extending the time allotted for completion. This approach not only engages the employee in problem-solving but also provides the leader with alternatives that balance organizational needs and individual capacity.

This three-step process has proved invaluable in my various careers. It exemplifies the main idea in Kenneth H. Blanchard's book *The One Minute Manager Meets the Monkey*. Instead of taking "monkeys on their backs" from their employees, Blanchard says leaders should empower people to imagine solutions.

I have used this lesson many times in the military as well as in business and education. I would ask new leaders to walk the halls of their organizations, moving from one area of responsibility to another. When they returned, I asked just one question: "How many monkeys climbed onto your back?" At first, most were confused. Then I explained: Each monkey represents a task or problem handed to them by an employee. The realization soon hit—by letting those monkeys climb aboard, leaders risk becoming weighed down with other people's responsibilities instead of empowering their teams to carry their own load.

As the new leader makes that walk, they quickly learn how easily casual hallway chats invite employees to hand off their "monkeys." Having risen from the ranks of most bureaucracies and being a "doer" and a "problem solver," the new boss is willing to take it on. The leader has taken the monkey off the back of their employee, but it's still a monkey. Avoid this temptation! Instead, take the following steps:

- Ask for a clear definition of the problem—the delineation of the problem, not the outcomes of the problem.
- Ask what steps they have taken to help resolve the issue that are within their control.
- Task out the responsibility (give back the monkey) by calling for a group to gather to prepare a prioritized list of options for the new leader to consider as part of the resolution.

This simple process has saved me more than once in challenging circumstances as a leader working on a transformation.

KEY INSIGHTS FROM CHAPTER FIVE
Transformations require urgency and belief in the need for change.

Data is a powerful catalyst for change. In APS, literacy and math scores declining over three years created a compelling case for immediate action. The challenge lies not in collecting data but in generating a shared sense of urgency that motivates stakeholders to act.

You can't turn the entire ship at once: Start with champions.

Identify proactive, respected leaders within the organization who are open to innovation and transformation. Empower these "early adopters"—especially principals—to pilot key changes and lead by example.

Champions become influencers when they achieve results.

When peer-respected leaders implement new strategies successfully, their results serve as proof points that quiet skeptics and inspire broader adoption. Change grows organically when credible leaders can articulate what's working and why.

Early initiatives need to be strategic, measurable, and impactful.

APS's transformation involved several impactful initiatives selected based on their potential to drive early wins and generate visible results:

- New literacy programs (K-12)
- Pacing guides
- Data walls
- Interim assessments
- 5th Block (targeted summer learning by invitation)

Transformation requires strategic piloting and iteration.

Not all programs were implemented district-wide immediately. Instead, they were launched in pockets through committed leaders, tested, and refined before broader adoption. This allowed for data collection, program refinement, and organic buy-in.

Peer-to-peer advocacy builds ownership and legitimacy.

Champions must be more than implementers—they should be empowered to *communicate* value to peers. Their voice is often more influential than top-down directives.

Courage and constructive dissent are essential in champions.

Champions must feel safe calling out shortcomings of an initiative while also being visionary enough to push for continuous improvement. Leaders must value feedback while still making timely decisions in the absence of perfect data.

Don't wait for complete certainty.

Action must sometimes be taken without complete information or guaranteed success. Leaders must be willing to move forward based on strong evidence and informed judgment—not paralyzed by analysis.

Institutionalize learning through data and reflection.

Every initiative should have mechanisms for tracking effectiveness (e.g., data walls, interim assessments, Professional Learning Communities). Programs that fail to deliver measurable outcomes should be acknowledged as such, and the organization must have the courage to pivot.

Credibility, not just compliance, drives sustainable change.

Transformational change lasts when it is built on trust, credibility, and demonstrated success—not compliance or coercion.

CHAPTER QUESTIONS TO CONSIDER

1. **Reflection on Leadership:** Who in your organization could be a champion for the transformative changes you envision? What qualities do these individuals possess that would make them effective leaders in this effort?
2. **Evaluating Current Data:** What data do you currently have that supports the need for change in your organization? How can you use this data to build urgency and momentum for the transformation?
3. **Building Momentum:** How do you plan to develop and sustain momentum for change in your

organization? What strategies could you implement to keep the urgency alive?

4. **Involving Stakeholders:** How can you involve key stakeholders, such as principals or department heads, in leading the change? What steps will you take to ensure they are empowered and supported in this role?

5. **Dealing with Resistance:** What are some potential sources of resistance to the changes you want to implement? How will you address these challenges to ensure the success of your initiatives?

6. **Resource Allocation:** How can you identify and allocate resources effectively to support your strategic initiatives? Are there areas in your current budget that could be reallocated to fund these efforts?

7. **Monitoring Progress:** How will you measure the success of the initiatives led by your champions? What indicators will you use to determine whether the changes are having the desired impact?

8. **Managing Capacity:** How do you determine the capacity for change within your organization? What strategies will you use to ensure that your team can handle the changes without becoming overwhelmed?

CHAPTER SIX

Owning Inputs and Outputs

Shortly after I started as superintendent of Aurora Public Schools (APS), I inquired about the evaluation process we had for employees. As I became more familiar with the various processes for the employee groups, it became obvious to me there was a severe lack of evaluation regarding outputs and an overwhelming priority given to inputs.

Here's what I mean. When teachers were evaluated, the Master Agreement, the negotiated document between the school district and the teacher's union, stated that non-tenured teachers (probationary teachers) would be evaluated once a year but tenured teachers (non-probationary teachers) would only be evaluated once every three years. First, not evaluating employees once a year seemed very strange to me but what really got my attention was that teacher evaluations were not connected to student outcomes—not even 1 percent of the evaluation included student achievement!

If a teacher did a good job in classroom management, connecting to parents, and preparing lessons they would be graded as being successful regardless of whether students were learning. The evaluation focus was on teaching rather than on learning. I could point to 95 percent of the teachers in the school district who were doing amazing work and getting terrific outcomes with students. But the system didn't allow us to recognize them or identify the ones that were not making the student gains we needed.

In business, if a segment of the company was not profitable, there would be major changes. In the military, we spent a lot of time on measured outcomes. In fact, in the United States Air Force, there was a strong movement to measure success by "effects-based" outcomes—a concept from military strategy in which success is measured by the actual impact of actions, not just by the completion of tasks or the outputs themselves. This was the culture that aligned with my values and strength. Not including student achievement in a teacher evaluation seemed outrageous to me.

I was also surprised by the culture in public education. I remember discussing the aspect of selecting teachers and principals of the year in our school district. The teachers' union pushed back, saying that in K-12 education all principals and teachers were treated equally and that no one should stand out. This was another shock to me. How could teachers new to the profession know whom to go to for advice if there was no way to find out the individuals who were excellent in their job as teachers? How could new principals know whom to get advice from if there was no way to know who were the best principals?

Interestingly, there were state and national competitions for best principal and teacher of the year, but the culture at APS and other school districts in Colorado did not help promote the effort. Without an outcome focus, selecting outstanding performers was very difficult. This needed to change.

We ultimately addressed this issue by ensuring that outstanding educators were recognized at the school level. In schools where principals took a proactive role, Teachers of the Year were celebrated openly, giving their colleagues visible role models to learn from. This not only honored excellence but also created a pathway for new teachers and principals to know whom to turn to for guidance. By making excellence visible, we began to shift the culture from one of uniformity to one that valued and elevated the very best within our schools.

Unions

While I was growing up in the Bronx and attending K-12 schools, I repeatedly heard the name Albert Shanker on the TV and radio. Even then, I knew he was a leader in education and heard about the work he did for teachers. As I have come to understand, Al Shanker founded the United Federation of Teachers and led the organization from 1964 to 1985, in addition to being president of the American Federation of

Teachers from 1974 to 1997. He was an activist for teachers and a prolific columnist for the *New York Times*.

Many of my family members were union members of the police department and the docks in New York City. While there are many controversies around unions, I am not anti-union. In fact, each year as superintendent in APS, I spoke to the 200 to 250 new teachers we hired every school year and encouraged them to join the teachers' union in our school district. I believe there is a role for unions in advocating for teachers; a union can provide a great service for superintendents in helping to prioritize the work of the school district.

However, as is often the case in history, there are times where priorities and leadership stray from what is correct and right. In the case of teacher unions, I have learned there is too much focus on the teachers and not enough focus on the students. I have met very few teachers who would say they don't put their students first; I had seen their devotion to students every day as superintendent. But the leadership of unions has wandered away from the focus on students and concentrated too much on adults. In my opinion, this is not what Al Shanker would support if he were alive today. I was taken aback when I had a leader of our teacher's union tell me that her role was to take care of the teachers and that if they were happy the students would learn. This is backwards! If the students are learning, teachers are happy, parents are happy, and, most importantly, students are happy and proud. Student learning is the outcome that counts.

If this rationale were applied to business, it would be like a leader saying that profit was not important if the employees are happy. Or, in the military, the focus would be on morale rather than on combat capability. There is a core competency that must be recognized in education and that is the ability to ensure our students learn. If the teaching is not getting what is needed in closing achievement gaps with challenged student populations or increasing student achievement for all, we need to recognize that and change our priorities. This was why we developed data walls in every school.

School Boards

There are different models in the United States where boards of education are concerned. Most of the large capital cities in our nation have mayoral control, but the more prevalent structure is elected boards of education. While there are various arguments on the pros and cons of both models, I am still supportive of local control by boards of education.

Mayoral control might be more efficient, but it is dependent on the relationship the superintendent has with one elected official that can change quickly because of a falling out or loss of election for the mayor. Boards of education are less efficient but more stable if the superintendent can maintain a majority of support.

I believe I can comfortably say that less than 1 percent of United States citizens have had the courage to put their names on a ballot for elected office in the history of our country. Add the fact that school board members almost never receive a salary for the long hours they put in for students in the nation, and you begin to understand the commitment that they have for students in K-12 education.

Of the various means of organizing boards, there is one that I recommend for school districts. John Carver has written many books on policy governance to empower boards of directors to fulfill their obligation of accountability for the organizations they govern.

As mentioned in Chapter Three, strategy is defined as connecting ends with means. John Carver's philosophy uses some of the same elements in his paradigm since his unique approach to policy governance focuses on organizational purposes (*ends*) from all other organizational issues (*means*).

One of the areas in the Carver model that deserves a lot of attention is the board of education and superintendent relationship. Carver works this area in negative terms; for example, "the superintendent will not put the financial security of the district at risk." The next level would be the "superintendent will not commit the district to any contract over $700,000 without the board approval." Now, the board has the authority to delve down to any level they want, even down to writing the checks (they would be hard-pressed to find a superintendent that would accept a position with that level of micro-management). But the real advantage of working this way is for the board and superintendent to know where the lines of authority rest, resulting in very little confusion. The board can change the lines of authority, but they should not do it retroactively when the superintendent has the authority to make a particular decision.

One way to describe governance is to visualize a line of governance where the board is above the line and the superintendent is below the line. Above the line, the board is responsible for policies, budgets, strategic plans, and hiring and firing their only employee, the superintendent. The superintendent's responsibilities are mostly below the line with operational responsibility for the day-to-day, week-to-week, and month-to-month of the school district in fulfilling polices, budgets, and the strategic plan. However, the superintendent must go above the line with the board as their single employee; the board members should not go below the line.

The challenge for boards of education is when they stray from a focus on ends and devote too much attention to means or the operational work of school districts. I have seen that happen in APS and other districts in the state and nation where a focus on outcomes is relegated to a focus on inputs. This is where boards make their biggest mistakes.

The most important job for a board of education is hiring the superintendent. The superintendent is their only employee and main contact with the school district. While any citizen can talk to any elected official, contacting or communicating with employees who try to represent district operations without going through the superintendent is detrimental to the efficient and effective workings of a school system.

I am also struck by the misconception that boards need to know everything that is going on in the district. As superintendent, I did not know everything that was going on every minute of every day! The ability to run a large organization depends on delegation and accountability. When district boards start talking about the "price of milk," as one of our board members would say, they are dealing too far down in the micro-management arena and not spending enough time on the policies and goals of the district. A board member is not failing if a constituent asks a question and they do not know the answer. The simple commitment is that the board member will get back to the citizen with an answer—and that is what I did anytime I did not know the answer to a question. It is very simple and respectful, but you are obligated to get back to that person.

The focus of boards of education should be on the "ends" of accelerating student achievement and closing the achievement gaps. This is where they need to hold the superintendent accountable, not on how the technology works in a particular school or how professional learning will be conducted at a particular grade level.

It is my opinion that boards of education should not meet more than once a month for about four hours—if business cannot be done during this time, the board needs to hold the superintendent accountable or take a hard look at their meeting agendas. Board workshops that include community attendance should be done additionally as needed but only in the interest of furthering the goals and ends of the district.

One of the best descriptions of relationships between school boards and superintendents is by Don McAdams in his book *What School Boards Can Do*:

> School boards and superintendents are partners, but they are not equal partners. Boards govern. Superintendents manage. Governance always trumps management. Governance is the trusteeship of power on behalf of the owners of power; management is the exercise of power under the oversight of governance.... Simply put, governance is steering; management is rowing. Governance is deciding what is to be done; management is doing it. In a democracy, governance must be broadly shared. Management responsibility needs to be concentrated in individuals.

KEY INSIGHTS FROM CHAPTER SIX

Evaluation culture should be aligned with student outcomes.

- Teacher evaluations in APS incorrectly prioritized inputs (e.g., lesson plans, classroom management) over outputs (student learning).
- Tenured teachers were only evaluated every three years, and student achievement was not factored into evaluations.

- The system failed to distinguish or recognize high-performing educators and did not provide mechanisms for improvement for those falling short.

There was cultural resistance to differentiation and recognition.

- There was a prevailing belief that all educators should be treated equally, which discouraged naming teacher or principal of the year.
- This hindered mentorship, as new educators had no clear model of excellence to learn from.
- Recognition of top performers is crucial to improvement, morale, and professional growth, but was resisted culturally.

Unions must balance adult and student interests.
True success lies in putting student learning first, which in turn leads to fulfillment for teachers and satisfaction for parents.

Governance should be outcome-focused.

- Boards of education often drift into operational details, losing sight of their main role: setting goals (*ends*) and holding superintendents accountable.
- The Carver model of policy governance emphasizes clear boundaries between governance and management.

- Micro-management by boards undermines effectiveness; their focus should stay on policies, student outcomes, strategic direction, budgets, and superintendent performance.

The relationship between the board and superintendent is pivotal.

- Boards have one employee: the superintendent. Their success is measured by student outcomes, not micro-management.
- Board members don't need to know every detail; their value lies in oversight, policy, and long-term strategic thinking.
- Time and energy should go to accelerating achievement and closing gaps, not operational minutiae like milk prices or tech issues.

Governance vs. Management

- Governance is steering; management is rowing.
- Boards govern; superintendents manage.
- Governance must be shared democratically; management must be concentrated for efficiency and accountability.

CHAPTER QUESTIONS TO CONSIDER

1. How do you think a focus on student outcomes could change the culture of teaching and learning in schools?

2. What role should teacher evaluations play in ensuring student success, and how might they be improved?

3. How can school boards balance their governance responsibilities with a focus on outcomes rather than micro-managing day-to-day operations?

4. In your experience, what are the risks and benefits of prioritizing outcomes over inputs in education?

5. How might unions and educational leaders collaborate to refocus efforts on student achievement while still supporting teachers?

6. What strategies could be implemented to better identify and recognize outstanding teachers and principals?

7. What are the potential challenges in shifting a school district's culture from input focused to outcome focused? How might these be addressed?

PART TWO

External Transformation

CHAPTER SEVEN

Generating Community Ownership

VISTA 2010 centered on outreach to students, staff, parents, and the broader community to identify clear expectations for student success, laying the groundwork for an internal, foundational transformation. The next phase—VISTA 2015—advanced the district to a higher level of external engagement with organizations beyond the school system, emphasizing shared ownership of students' success across the community. While parents involved in politics, business, and local affairs already paid attention to school results, the goal was to widen that circle so the entire community—not just parents—assumed responsibility for the district's outcomes. The 2006 listening tour for VISTA 2010 had asked partners how they could support the district's needs (an internal focus). By contrast, during the 2011 listening tour for the new strategic plan, VISTA 2015 asked what the community needed so that, working together, everyone could prepare students for college, careers, and success in life (an external focus).

As a result, a Community Workforce Planning Team (CWPT) was formed. It was a public-private partnership involving more than thirty community groups and organizations representing higher education, industry, economic development, workforce development, and the school district. The goal was to align academic pathways with local workforce needs to improve the future of APS students and the surrounding community.

I believe that in the twentieth century, economic and academic development drifted apart, but in the twenty-first century they must advance in tandem. When this vision is shared with external partners—especially businesses—it resonates immediately. The central idea is that every partner should see a return on their investment of time, expertise, and resources, rather than viewing collaboration as philanthropy alone. What makes this effort unique is that it is community-led, designed to create and implement meaningful pathways that expand postsecondary opportunities and strengthen workforce readiness for APS graduates—built entirely on shared interests.

The CWPT developed a Community Workforce Plan that was the cornerstone for developing academic and career pathways across the school district to align academic and economic development. The CWPT considered input from focus groups conducted in spring 2010 as well as the expertise and experience of its members to develop the plan. Goals for setting up a CWPT are:

- Developing and monitoring pathway-specific advisory committees charged with ensuring high, consistent standards for implementation, maintenance, and evaluation for all pathways.
- Identifying and helping students connect early to relevant curriculum, career, and training opportunities and resources in each academic and career pathway.
- Connecting students to advantages that will help them compete locally, nationally, and globally in high-demand, high-skill, and high-paying careers.
- Building strong partnerships among all groups within the CWPT alliance to benefit students, local industries/career sectors, and the community at large.
- Providing the community access to a locally developed and qualified workforce that is aligned with employer expectations.
- Responding to changing industry needs to sustain current and emerging workforce demands.

In alignment with the CWPT, a goal in the APS strategic plan (VISTA 2015) was to have at least one academic and career pathway in every school by 2015. Additionally, beginning in 2011, every sixth-grade APS student would have an Individual Career and Academic Plan to guide them in setting career and academic goals.

It's important to build pathways for student choice and community involvement where companies can do more than write a check; they can promote their discipline and plant the seeds for future employees.

Own the Concept of a Postsecondary Workforce Readiness Focus

To prepare students for the twenty-first century, school districts and communities must work together to create a seamless P–20 system, stretching from preschool through higher education. In this framework, high school graduation is not the finish line but rather a gateway. For those students who choose education beyond high school—whether undergraduate or postgraduate study—academic and career pathways provide the structure to expand their options, strengthen workforce readiness, and ensure they can make meaningful choices about their future.

When students are motivated through practical, relevant learning in their areas of career interest, student achievement increases. Students develop academic, technical, and workforce readiness skills that prepare them for high-demand, high-skill, and high-paying jobs. In addition to preparing students for college and the workforce, academic and career pathways offer students the opportunity to earn industry certificates (e.g., Microsoft, Cisco), Occupational Safety and Health Administration certification, college credit, pilot/drone pilot/aircraft mechanic certificates, and even associate's degrees while they are still in high school.

With the help of external partners in the community, school districts need to change the twentieth-century industrial model to a twenty-first-century system of critical thinking, creativity, communication, and collaboration that provides energy and excitement for learning organized around postsecondary and workforce readiness. Our students become "academic journeymen" connected to the real world and better prepared for the future they choose by understanding the application—not just the acquisition—of knowledge.

As part of twenty-first-century learning, APS created Vista PEAK, a P-20-focused campus that serves students from preschool through postsecondary. It was the district's first P-20 model with four academic and career pathways to develop students' academic, technical, and employability skills. This 100-acre site provided a seamless continuum of public education with dedicated space for preschool, a state-of-the-art K-8, and a high school where students could enroll in college courses to earn dual credit to prepare them to pursue a wide variety of educational choices.

Throughout the district, we explored ways to develop new schools and organize existing schools to better support expanded educational opportunities and choice. The one-size-fits-all approach from the industrial age way of learning needed to be replaced by opportunities or pathways that better match schools with diverse student learning needs and interests.

Engage Outside Collaboration to Further Student Achievement

Colorado faces a paradox that complicates the conversation on educational reform. Though not unique to the state, it underscores why both internal and external transformation are essential within the P–20 framework. Despite ranking second in the nation for adults with college degrees, Colorado ranks 47th in the percentage of high school graduates who continue on to college, according to the Free Application for Federal Student Aid (FAFSA). In effect, the state imports much of its educated workforce—a dynamic that Aurora Public Schools became determined to change.

APS teamed up with more than thirty groups and organizations throughout the community and created a five-year plan that aligned APS's academic and career pathways with industry demands and postsecondary requirements. Through this Community Workforce Planning Team, APS and the community created four academic and career pathways, each of which provides students with rigorous curricula connected with focused, hands-on, relevant learning and postsecondary and workforce readiness skills. The four pathways that APS selected are:

- Health Sciences: Prepares students to pursue rewarding careers in over 150 medical and allied career fields.
- Science, Technology, Engineering, and Math (STEM): Prepares students to enter careers in any of the four parts of STEM.

- Business: Prepares students for careers in financial services, accounting, business administration, marketing, and business support services.
- Arts and Communications: Prepares students for careers in the arts, teaching, media, and communication.

Each of these pathways had partnerships with various organizations, such as the Anschutz Medical Center for the health sciences pathway, aerospace companies like Lockheed Martin for STEM, Alpine banks for business, and the Denver Center for Performing Arts for arts/communications. Through these partnerships, APS had the ability to give students real-life experiences outside of the classroom. Instead of just going to organizations in the community and asking for a check, a school district can enhance community involvement with schools by offering opportunities for:

- Internships
- Externships
- Job shadowing
- Mentoring
- Jobs, if the students are old enough

I was quoted numerous times stating: "We need to make sure we're offering opportunities for our kids who are growing up within the state of Colorado. So, through this CWPT pathways program and our P-20 concept, we are aligning academic and economic development and targeting the Colorado paradox." These pathways provide countless benefits to students. Academic and career pathways increase student achievement because students are motivated through practical, relevant learning in their areas of career interest. Through these pathways, students develop academic, technical, and workforce readiness skills that prepare them for life after high school graduation. They may even earn industry certificates, college credit, or an associate's degree while still in high school.

These pathways give students the chance to explore various fields and career pathways and they give them motivation about the professions they can be aligned with in the city, state, and nation. If we truly want to be globally competitive, then we must partner as a community to give our students real-life experiences and get them excited about their future professions.

In 2010, APS set out to define a five-year plan to align academic and economic development. An outside consulting firm was hired to survey the economic needs of the Aurora and general Denver metro area regarding employment opportunities for that year and the next decade. Armed with this information, APS and the CWPT were able to draft a five-year plan for the external transformation.

Strategy continued to be the manner of transformation by connecting ends with means so a vision (*ends*) was devised and goals (*means*) were written as a subset of the overall VISTA 2015 strategic plan. This second five-year strategic plan shifted focus to external engagement, aligning educational outcomes with workforce and community needs to ensure student success in postsecondary education and careers. A mission and core values were devised to further expand the understanding of this external effort. The *vision* was to:

> *Meet local workforce needs by connecting resources from industry through postsecondary education to ensure seamless, engaging, and replicable academic and career pathways. These pathways prepare all Aurora Public Schools students for superior academic success and employment advancement in their chosen careers.*

The *mission* became:

> *In pursuit of its vision, the Community Workforce Planning Team is dedicated to collaborative strategic development that aligns economic and educational initiatives for the benefit of students, local industries, and the entire community.*

Core values were developed as a cultural framework for development:

- Students are motivated by aligned curriculum and training—based on the needs of local businesses and industries—that provide a superior academic foundation and marketable skill sets that prepare students for success in higher education and the workforce.

- Business and industries gain access to a valuable, locally developed, and certified talent pool. This reduces recruitment and training costs and increases workforce productivity.
- Higher education strengthens its connections with preschool through 12th grade and business/industry partners through articulation agreement that align secondary, postsecondary, and career-based programs of study through seamless pathway curricula.
- The community is stronger and healthier when students have options to stay in their hometown. The community gains a qualified workforce, economic growth, and intergenerational relationships.

In the spring of 2010, more than forty career professionals representing all the four pathways met and participated in a discussion of how to create a viable and sustainable pipeline that would align educational efforts with community workforce needs. This is how the Community Workforce Readiness Planning Team began.

The CWPT was an alliance of more than thirty community groups and organizations representing higher education, industry, economic development, workforce development, and APS.

One of the major focus elements for the alliance was to reverse the Colorado paradox by creating a five-year plan that aligned APS's academic and career pathways with industry demands and postsecondary requirements. The exciting insight the CWPT gained was that students in pathway programs learn marketable skills so they are prepared for successful entry into higher education and the workforce.

Academic and career pathways drive student achievement by giving young people ownership of their learning. When students can choose pathways aligned with their career interests, they are motivated to engage deeply in relevant academics and skill-building. Through these pathways, students develop academic, technical, and workforce readiness skills that prepare them for high-demand, high-skill, and high-paying careers. The community benefits as well, gaining a pipeline of future employees equipped with the competencies local industries need.

These pathways are intentionally sequenced across grade levels:

- ACCESS (Elementary School): Students build a foundation in core academics while being introduced to broad occupational categories. Teachers differentiate instruction based on interests, and students begin exploring pathways through activities such as field trips, exposure to the four pathways, and early visits to college campuses.
- EXPLORE (Middle School): Students delve deeper into career clusters, continue exposure to all four pathways, and begin to identify specific courses and experiences that align with their developing interests.

- PREPARE (High School): Students focus on their chosen pathways, with opportunities for real-world engagement through part-time employment, internships, job shadowing, workshops, seminars, summer programs, mentorships, guest speakers, and other field experiences.

All four academic and career pathways—Health Sciences, STEM, Business, and Arts and Communications—provide students with rigorous curricula connected with focused, hands-on, relevant learning and postsecondary and workforce readiness skills.

A CWPT's five-year plan can become the cornerstone for the development of academic and career pathways. The unique community-led effort can provide graduates with meaningful postsecondary choices and workforce readiness skills. A CWPT five-year plan should focus on the following key goals:

- Identifying community educational and workforce needs
- Improving educational outcomes
- Involving industry with education
- Increasing employment opportunities

The initial focus-group feedback provided current and relevant input to a comprehensive assessment of the Aurora workforce environment. It highlighted potential gaps between industry needs and the availability of qualified workers. When developing the five-year plan, the CWPT identified existing community assets and additional resources that were needed to meet local workforce needs.

In February 2011, the CWPT presented the Academic and Career Pathways Five-Year Plan to the APS Board of Education and appropriate partner boards. The CWPT met on a semi-annual basis to oversee the implementation of the plan. A CWPT should be committed to its vision of meeting local needs and preparing all students in the community for superior academic success and employment advancement in their chosen careers.

KEY INSIGHTS FROM CHAPTER SEVEN

Transformation must move beyond the school walls.

- **VISTA 2010** initiated change by focusing internally: students, staff, and families.
- **VISTA 2015** expanded the mission to include external community stakeholders in student success.
- A successful school district transformation requires community-wide ownership, not just parental involvement.

Strategic listening evolves over time.

- Early listening tours asked how the community could support the district.

- Later tours flipped the question—asking what the *community needed* to thrive and how schools could contribute.
- This pivot from internal to external listening redefined community engagement and educational relevance.

The Community Workforce Planning Team was a game-changer.

- The CWPT was formed as a *public-private alliance* with more than thirty organizations across sectors.
- The CWPT focused on aligning academic goals with *economic development* and workforce needs.
- The CWPT became the engine behind developing *career pathways* and *postsecondary readiness.*

Economic and academic development must be joined.

- In the twentieth century, education and workforce preparation were siloed.
- For the twenty-first century, schools must *integrate academic and economic goals*, creating shared outcomes with business and industry.
- While philanthropy is helpful, *mutual benefit and return on investment for all partners* makes the model sustainable.

Academic and career pathways create student motivation and workforce readiness.

- Students are more motivated when learning is *relevant* and *aligned with career interests.*
- Pathways provide academic, technical, and employability skills for *high-demand, high-wage careers.*
- Students can earn industry certifications, college credits, and even associate degrees *while still in high school.*

Education must become a P-20 system.

- High school graduation isn't the finish line.
- Students must be supported from preschool through postsecondary (P-20).
- The Vista PEAK P-20 campus provided a living model of this seamless continuum.

Invest in local students for the long-term.

- Colorado imports college-educated workers due to low in-state college continuation rates. APS made it a mission to reverse this trend by investing in local students through career pathways and partnerships.

Collaboration enhances student experiences beyond the classroom.

- Partnerships provide access to internships, externships, job shadowing, mentorship, and employment.

- Companies don't just fund programs; they cultivate local talent.

The ACCESS–EXPLORE–PREPARE framework makes pathways tangible.

- **ACCESS** (elementary): Introduces students to career concepts and pathways.
- **EXPLORE** (middle school): Lets students investigate various careers and begin focused learning.
- **PREPARE** (high school): Offers hands-on experiences, certifications, and real-world connections.

Strategy and structure enable systemic change.

- Strategy connects ends (*vision*) with means (*goals and implementation*).
- CWPT's five-year plan provided the structural backbone for district-wide alignment.
- A shared vision, mission, and core values drove unified purpose across sectors.

CHAPTER QUESTIONS TO CONSIDER

1. How can your local community become more involved in supporting the success of students in your school district?
2. What steps can you take to foster collaboration between schools and local industries to align educational outcomes with workforce needs?

3. How might your school district benefit from forming a public-private alliance like the Community Workforce Planning Team?
4. In what ways can academic and career pathways enhance student motivation and achievement in your community?
5. What challenges do you foresee in shifting from an internal to an external focus in your educational initiatives? How might these challenges be addressed?
6. How does your school district currently engage with external partners, and what opportunities exist to expand these relationships?
7. What role do you believe the broader community should play in preparing students for postsecondary success and workforce readiness?
8. How can you ensure that the benefits of community involvement in education are felt by all students, regardless of their background or circumstances?

CHAPTER EIGHT

Owning the Need for External Learning Opportunities

School districts cannot carry the weight of preparing students for the twenty-first century alone. While they are central to the education process, they are only one part of a much larger ecosystem of support that shapes a child's growth, opportunity, and ultimate success. Communities are filled with organizations—youth-serving nonprofits, museums, afterschool programs, and civic institutions—that bring expertise, resources, and inspiration into young people's lives. When schools embrace these **External Learning Opportunities (ELOs)** and intentionally connect them with student pathways, they expand learning beyond the classroom walls and create new engines of motivation, ownership, and achievement.

This chapter is important to *Super Ownership* because it demonstrates that true transformation requires both internal reforms within schools and external partnerships across communities. By integrating ELOs into a district's vision, schools can give students not only the academic foundation they need but also the real-world experiences, mentorships, and exposures that fuel purpose and drive. When students see how their education connects to future opportunities, they take ownership of their learning, and that ownership becomes the engine of success.

My own leadership journey confirmed this lesson. After serving as superintendent of Aurora Public Schools (APS) for seven years, I transitioned into leading two very different but deeply connected organizations: the Boys & Girls Clubs of Metro Denver (BCGMD) and Wings Over the Rockies Air & Space Museum (WOTR). Both experiences taught me that when communities step up to co-own the educational mission, schools no longer stand isolated. Instead, they become part of a woven fabric of opportunity—one that nurtures student growth, prepares young people for college and a career, and ensures our nation remains globally competitive.

External Learning Opportunities: Boys & Girls Clubs

After serving as the superintendent of APS, I embarked on another nontraditional endeavor: becoming CEO of the BGCMD. This put me in a nonprofit environment for youth development and allowed me to exercise and commit to my understanding of the value to young people of ELOs, such as educational programs, experiences, and support offered by organizations such as community centers, museums, and after-school programs. To move from mere partnership to genuine integration, I led an initiative to embed club programs directly inside schools as after-hours extensions of the school day. By co-locating BGCMD staff on campus, aligning activities with district curricula, and sharing outcome goals, we turned "after-school" into "after-hours learning"—a seamless bridge between classroom objectives and youth development supports.

This case study is another example on how ownership by other external organizations committed to student enhancements can contribute to the external transformation discussion. I have reflected many times on the need for partnerships outside of K-12 education to enhance our ability to be globally competitive in the twenty-first century, and here was an opportunity to take what I learned at APS and strengthen the bridge between schools and the successful youth development organization of Boys & Girls Clubs. Integrating clubs into school facilities accelerated that bridge. It enabled shared attendance data (with appropriate agreements), coordinated academic supports, and allowed consistent mentoring from the last bell through the early evening—all in the same, familiar setting for students and families.

If my premise that schools and ELOs are essential for the United States to be competitive globally, then the

BGCMD would allow me to expand on the theory that choice equals ownership, ownership equals motivation, and motivation equals success. The Boys & Girls Clubs of America are made up of 1,140 independent organizations with 4,100 club locations, impacting nearly 4 million children and teens throughout the nation through the commitment that "Every child deserves a great future." At BGCMD we had fifteen clubs serving more than 8,000 club members in the Denver metro area. Like I did at APS, I approached this new position by starting with a ninety-day listening tour and setting up the development of a five-year strategic plan.

Within the humble yet vibrant walls of the Boys & Girls Clubs, a vision for transformation was unveiled. It was a vision to empower lives, to strengthen communities, and to ignite the flames of ambition and resilience in the hearts of every member who walked through its doors. Enshrined in our mission was a pledge to every member: to graduate high school with a plan for college or career, to contribute to their community, and to live a healthy life. This was more than a mere mission statement; it was a promise to nurture the potential of each member, guiding them toward a future filled with hope and opportunity.

At the core of this vision were the values that would guide every action and decision: respect, integrity, excellence, teamwork, and innovation. These were not just words on a page but principles that would shape the very fabric of the Boys & Girls Clubs, ensuring that every interaction, program, and initiative was grounded in integrity and driven by a commitment to excellence.

As the foundation of this grand vision, the strategic pillars were laid bare, each one a testament to the organization's unwavering dedication to its members and their communities. From fostering a positive environment and experience to embracing continuous evaluation and innovation, these pillars formed the bedrock upon which the clubs' future would be built. Under Environment, school-based clubs prioritized safe, trusted spaces within the very schools students already knew, reducing transportation barriers and increasing consistent participation. Under Academics and Career, we mapped club activities to district standards and pathway themes, ensuring tutoring, STEM labs, arts, and leadership programs reinforced what students were learning during the day.

Trust was the cornerstone of this vision, underpinning every aspect of the organization's operations. From managing finances with integrity to recruiting and retaining the highest quality staff and volunteers, trust was not just earned but cherished as the lifeblood of the club's existence. But trust alone wasn't enough. The club also recognized the importance of operating within its means and guidelines, ensuring financial sustainability and accountability while diversifying and innovating new funding streams to support its mission.

Environment was another key pillar of the organization's vision, with a focus on creating safe and supportive spaces where each member could thrive. From ensuring emotional and physical safety to strengthening collaboration with parents and schools, the clubs sought to reach beyond their walls to create a network of support for their members.

Academics and career development were central to the Clubs' mission, with a commitment to providing impactful experiences that would set every member on the path to success. From preventing summer learning loss to preparing teen members for post–high school education and careers, the clubs aimed to equip every member with the skills and resources they needed to achieve their dreams.

Character and leadership were also paramount, with a focus on developing strong character and leadership skills that would empower every member to become leaders in their communities, both in action and example.

Finally, **wellness** was a fundamental aspect of the organization's vision, with a focus on promoting healthy lifestyles and avoiding high-risk behaviors. From encouraging regular exercise and healthy eating to providing education on sexual health and substance abuse prevention, the clubs aimed to empower every member to take responsibility for their health and well-being.

As the vision for the Boys & Girls Clubs unfolded, it became clear that this was more than just a club; it was a movement, a force for positive change in the lives of countless individuals and communities across the nation. And as the journey began, so too did the promise of a brighter future for all who dared to dream.

Over the past decade, BGCMD committed to, pursued, and achieved "Growth with Impact." Since 2007, we have expanded our service sites from seven to seventeen, resulting in a 136 percent increase in the number of youth served each day. Throughout our expansion efforts, we have enjoyed exceptional financial support and stability, allowing us to evaluate our impact, capture and replicate best practices, and identify opportunities for improvement. A key driver of that impact was the school-embedded Club model, which increased daily attendance, improved handoffs between teachers and youth-development staff, and expanded family engagement through on-site evening events and services.

As a result, we have emphasized twenty-first-century skills such as communication, collaboration, creativity, and critical thinking, which will be essential to our club members' ability to succeed in their education and career. We have committed to better engaging families and providing critical wraparound and support services to help families meet basic needs. Throughout all our efforts, we built and cultivated partnerships with other institutions in the communities we serve—schools, neighborhood coalitions, businesses, volunteer groups, community centers, police departments, and other organizations—to align our efforts around common goals and avoid duplication of services.

Today, BGCMD is one of the largest youth development organizations in metropolitan Denver and one of the largest

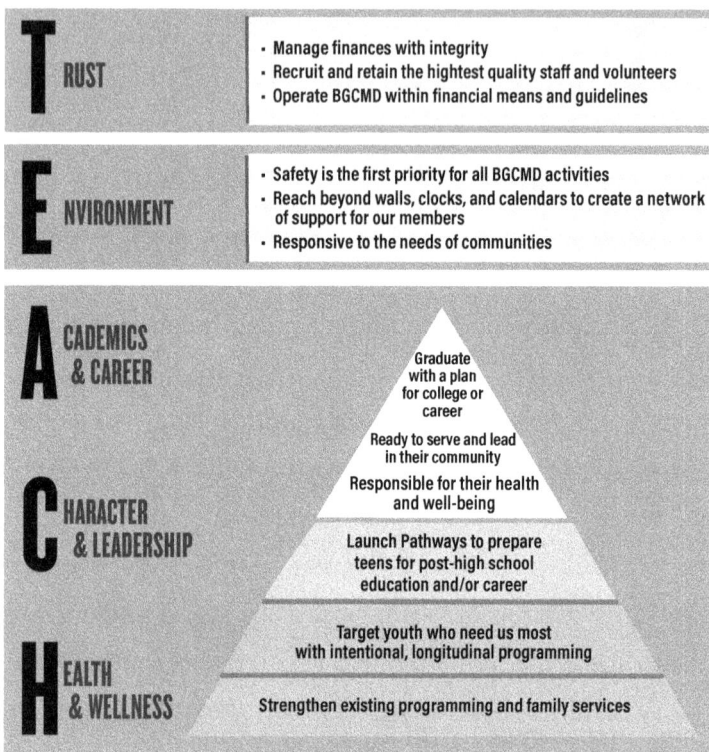

TRUST
- Manage finances with integrity
- Recruit and retain the hightest quality staff and volunteers
- Operate BGCMD within financial means and guidelines

ENVIRONMENT
- Safety is the first priority for all BGCMD activities
- Reach beyond walls, clocks, and calendars to create a network of support for our members
- Responsive to the needs of communities

ACADEMICS & CAREER

CHARACTER & LEADERSHIP

HEALTH & WELLNESS

Graduate with a plan for college or career

Ready to serve and lead in their community

Responsible for their health and well-being

Launch Pathways to prepare teens for post-high school education and/or career

Target youth who need us most with intentional, longitudinal programming

Strengthen existing programming and family services

BGCMD Strategic Plan Pillars

Boys & Girls Clubs across the country, with a highly diverse membership. However, we believed the time had come to shift our focus from growing our footprint in the community, to growing the effectiveness of our current services and increasing our impact on the club members who rely on us day after day.

As stated before, strategy is connecting ends with means. In the BGCMD IMPACT 2020 strategic plan, the end is the vision and our means are the goals/objectives/actions. By building on the pillars of Trust, Environment, Academic and Career, Character and Leadership, and Health and Wellness (TEACH), BGCMD created a strategic plan that aimed to have long-term impact on our club members and the Greater Denver community. The school-embedded model operationalized that strategy: ends (higher achievement, stronger readiness, safer communities) met means (shared facilities, unified goals, and coordinated staffing) in the same physical space.

Moving forward, we strove to increase our impact on our "highly engaged" club members—those who attended the clubs three times per week or more—through a targeted, outcomes-driven initiative. Past evaluation had proven that club programming is most impactful for those who attend and participate regularly, helping them succeed academically, make healthy choices, and lead and serve in their communities. Therefore, in our IMPACT 2020 plan we added an intentional approach to ensure that those youth who attend the clubs frequently reach specific benchmarks of self-sufficiency. This meant that BGCMD would move away from a focus on specific programs and activities and toward a focus on desired outcomes for individual club members. In the following years, we worked to:

- Implement new systems to track "cohorts" of youth over multiple years to better understand the highly engaged club member and how to match their individual needs with the right types of interventions.

- Develop improved networks of support for club members by increasing our connections with families, teachers, and other community partners.
- Improve services for all club members by:

  * Dedicating resources to provide support for families in need, including emergency funds and connections to community partners to prevent or relieve crises.
  * Providing more intensive training for all staff based on national best practices in youth development.
  * Identifying key skills, such as goal-setting, resilience, communication, problem-solving, and reflection and consistently focusing on developing them across all areas of the club through intentional activities and messaging.

Of course, as we were implementing IMPACT 2020, we continued to be an asset to the community by maintaining our comprehensive approach to youth development. We renewed our commitment to working with the whole child, year-round, and bridging the gap between school and home by working beyond the traditional school day to help young people learn and grow. We continued to be responsive to community needs, to measure our impact, and to continually adapt and improve our services based on what we learned. By bridging school and home on the same campus, the after-hours club became the continuity thread—a place where students could receive targeted academic help, explore pathway-aligned enrichment, and access wraparound services without leaving school grounds.

For more than fifty years, the Boys & Girls Club of Metro Denver had formed the bedrock of thousands of young people's paths to success. Along their journeys, the dedicated and professional staff members at our Clubs had been there, day in and day out, to help our young people learn and practice the skills, attitudes, and behaviors that have allowed them to persevere in the face of obstacles. Our Clubs were thriving. Inside each Club were hundreds of curious minds tackling new challenges, budding artists discovering their creativity, enthusiastic athletes channeling their energy, and friendly, engaged teens making plans to be the first in their family to graduate from college.

An investment in Boys & Girls Clubs of Metro Denver— which provides opportunities that help young people avoid costly mistakes and become self-sufficient adults—brings a sizeable economic return when our young people succeed. (A study conducted for Boys & Girls Clubs in Wisconsin in 2015 found that every $1 invested in the clubs returned $12.46 in economic benefits.) Our city became a home to club alumni who positively contributed to our society as judges, web designers, nurses, and business owners and in many other ways. They were once young club members, walking through our doors after school, talking about their day with our staff members and playing basketball on our courts. With our renewed and deepened commitment to our club members in the IMPACT 2020 plan, we hoped that others would join us in opening doors, expanding opportunity, and building great futures for thousands of children in the Denver area.

External Learning Opportunities: Wings Over the Rockies Museum

My next adventure, in 2017, was to become the President and CEO of the Wings Over the Rockies Air & Space Museum (WOTR), an aviation and space museum that educates the public about aviation history and inspires future generations to pursue careers in aerospace. I had been on the board for seven years and board chair for two years before serving as the president/CEO for eight years.

WOTR began as a follow-on to the long legacy of Lowry Air Force Base, which opened in 1937 and was in operation through World War II, the Korean War, and the Vietnam War. Lowry was one of the U.S. bases closed after the Cold War ended. In 1994, the United States Air Force entrusted a 100,000-plus-square-foot hangar to a newly christened institution: Wings Over the Rockies Museum. Spearheaded by a dedicated group of volunteers, the museum was initially started with aircraft loaned from the U.S. Air Force Museum. By 1997, WOTR had earned the prestigious designation as Colorado's official air and space museum. Over the ensuing years, the museum's offerings expanded significantly, encompassing a diverse array of spacecraft and civilian aircraft within its exhibits. In 2011, a significant renovation was unveiled, marked by the striking sight of the Boeing B-52 being elevated onto pedestals. Today, visitors flock to the museum to partake in an array of interactive experiences interspersed with world-class historical exhibits. With its steadfast commitment to growth and innovation, WOTR has ascended to global acclaim, standing proudly as one of the foremost aviation and space museums worldwide.

In 2014, WOTR broke ground on a second location, the Exploration of Flight campus at Centennial Airport, to extend the WOTR mission by providing interactive aviation and aerospace education. The campus includes exhibits, flight simulators, and the Colorado SKIES Academy, a middle school focused on aerospace education. The culmination of this endeavor was the opening of the EOF Campus in July 2018 with the Blue Sky Hangar, followed by the establishment of the Colorado SKIES Academy in 2019. Exploration of Flight serves as a vibrant hub for aerospace education, immersive experiences, and exhilarating fun. Visitors are invited to come to our expansive fifteen-acre campus and delve into the captivating world of aviation at the Blue Sky Aviation Gallery, where inspiration and education are inseparable. And on the horizon awaits the eagerly anticipated Ozmen Black Sky Space Gallery, poised to ignite curiosity and wonder in the realm of space exploration and education.

Building on the same philosophy that guided my work with the Boys & Girls Clubs, WOTR launched Wings

Aerospace Exploration (WAE) as an intentional ELO that gives students ownership of their learning through authentic, hands-on experiences. WAE serves students in grades 6–12, preparing them for potential careers in aerospace science, aerospace engineering, general aviation, or unmanned aircraft systems. The program is designed not to replace the regular school curriculum but rather to complement it as an enrichment pathway, where students explore RC airplanes, drones and robotics, coding, rocketry, and other aviation and space-related subjects.

Like embedding clubs into schools, WAE creates a bridge between classroom instruction and real-world application. Students engage with aerospace professionals, gain mentorship and exposure, and discover how their academic studies connect to future opportunities. By offering WAE at both Wings locations—the historic Lowry campus and the Exploration of Flight campus—WOTR ensures access for a wide range of students and families. In doing so, it demonstrates how museums and community organizations can co-own the mission of preparing students for meaningful futures, especially in high-demand fields like aerospace and aviation.

Today, both the Air & Space Museum at the old Lowry location and the Exploration of Flight campus on Centennial Airport buzz with activity, offering visitors access to state-of-the-art flight simulators, captivating interactive experiences, and unparalleled historical exhibits. With these two dynamic locations working in tandem—and the addition of WAE as a structured ELO—Wings Over the Rockies has solidified its reputation as one of the premier aviation and space organizations in the country, while also extending its impact directly into the lives of students preparing to chart their own pathways into the future.

When I took over as President/CEO, I embarked on the familiar track of doing a ninety-day listening tour and working on a transformational approach of developing a strategic plan much like I had done in Aurora Public Schools and the Denver Metro Boys & Girls Clubs. Developing vision, mission, values, and strategic pillars within six months, we had the makings of a road map for the future.

Closing

The lesson is clear: Schools cannot and should not try to transform alone. External learning opportunities are not an optional add-on but, rather, a critical part of how students discover purpose, gain ownership of their choices, and prepare for the world that awaits them. Partnerships with organizations like the Boys & Girls Clubs and Wings Over the Rockies illustrate how community assets, when aligned with schools, can dramatically expand the range of experiences and pathways available to students. These partnerships turn the abstract idea of "college and career readiness" into lived experiences and build confidence, competence, and vision for the future.

Beyond clubs and museums, districts can braid in a wide constellation of ELOs: public libraries and makerspaces;

YMCAs, 4-H, Scouts, and Civil Air Patrol/JROTC; community colleges for dual enrollment and industry certificates; trade unions and employers for pre-apprenticeships and paid internships; hospitals, clinics, and senior centers for health and human services rotations; parks, wildlife, and conservation corps for field science; police/fire/EMT Explorer posts and National Guard Youth Challenge programs for public safety pathways; arts councils, theaters, and music schools for creative careers; local startups and small businesses for entreneurship labs; faith- and service-based nonprofits for leadership and civic engagement; and virtual micro-internships, hackathons, and challenge-based competitions that connect students to mentors nationwide. The point is not to add noise but to curate high-quality partners that map to standards, earnable credentials, and real jobs—so every student can test interests, build mastery, and see a line of sight to adulthood.

If *Super Ownership* is about leaders taking responsibility for both internal and external transformation, then ELOs are the proving ground of that responsibility. They show what is possible when schools open their doors to the larger community and when the community, in turn, accepts co-ownership of student success. In the end, every great future is built not by schools or organizations working in isolation but by ecosystems of learning and opportunity working in concert. That is the kind of transformation required for the twenty-first century—and that is the promise we must deliver to every student.

KEY INSIGHTS FROM CHAPTER EIGHT

Schools cannot do it alone.

- School districts are only one part of the larger ecosystem supporting student development.
- Partnering with youth-focused community organizations is essential to address gaps in learning, access, and holistic growth.

External learning opportunities foster ownership, motivation, and success.

- When students are given choices through ELOs, they gain ownership of their learning, which enhances motivation and leads to better outcomes.
- This belief guided both my leadership at APS and my subsequent work at BGCMD WOTR.

BGCMD: A Case Study in Strategic Youth Development

- The Boys & Girls Clubs of Metro Denver serves as a model for how external organizations can deeply influence youth success.
- With a strategic plan rooted in **TEACH** (Trust, Environment, Academic and career, Character and leadership, Health and wellness), the clubs offer a values-driven, impact-focused experience.

- Growth with impact: We increased the number of club locations and youth served while strengthening services and measuring effectiveness.
- Emphasis on twenty-first-century skills, family engagement, wraparound support, and community collaboration.

Shift from program delivery to outcomes.

- BGCMD's IMPACT 2020 strategic plan moved from simply offering programs to targeting outcomes—focusing on *highly engaged members* who attend frequently.
- Introduced systems to track youth progress longitudinally, align resources, and prioritize development of skills like resilience, goal-setting, and communication.

Sustained community partnerships are crucial.

- Strategic partnerships with schools, neighborhoods, law enforcement, and businesses ensured services were complementary, not duplicative.
- Community-based organizations can and should help fill the space between school and home, especially after school hours.

Preserve and evolve a legacy of learning.

- Wings Over the Rockies is an example of how ELOs can also provide *inspiration and career pathways*, particularly in STEM and aviation.

- Born from the legacy of Lowry Air Force Base, the museum evolved into a globally recognized institution for aerospace education.

Dual Campus Model = Broader Reach

- The addition of Exploration of Flight at Centennial Airport expanded hands-on, immersive experiences in real-world aviation settings.
- The Blue Sky Aviation Gallery and the future Ozmen Black Sky Space Gallery connect young learners directly with aviation professionals, aircraft, and simulators.

Aerospace Education = Pathways to the Future

- Programs and exhibits encourage interest in aviation, engineering, and space—offering students unique pathways to explore career and academic opportunities beyond traditional classroom settings.
- WOTR not only preserves history but also prepares future aerospace leaders by providing dynamic, engaging, and inspiring experiences.

Strategic Leadership Insights

- Whether in a nonprofit youth organization or a museum, strategic planning is about *connecting ends with means.*

- Listening tours, mission clarity, values alignment, outcome focus, and adaptive systems are crucial to leading impactful organizations.
- External learning opportunities are essential, not just supplemental.
- ELOs must be *intentional*, *outcomes-driven*, and *aligned with broader community goals*.
- Embracing ELOs allows communities to reimagine what student success looks like and expand the definition of where, how, and with whom learning takes place.

CHAPTER QUESTIONS TO CONSIDER

1. Reflecting on your own experiences, how have external learning opportunities, such as those offered by community organizations, impacted your growth or the growth of those you know?
2. In what ways do you think schools can better integrate partnerships with organizations like Boys & Girls Clubs to enhance student learning and development?
3. What are the potential challenges you foresee in creating and maintaining successful collaborations between schools and external organizations? How might these challenges be addressed?
4. How do you believe giving students choices in their educational pathways affects their motivation and

overall success? Can you think of any examples where choice has made a difference?

5. Consider your own community: What external learning opportunities exist, and how might they be better leveraged to support youth development?

6. What role do you see community organizations playing in preparing students for the twenty-first-century workforce, and how can schools and organizations like WOTR and BGCMD collaborate to achieve this?

7. How might the principles of ownership, motivation, and success discussed in this chapter be applied to other areas of education or youth development?

CHAPTER NINE

Owning Crisis Management

Not all external partnerships emerge from enrichment opportunities or career pathways. Some are forged in tragedy. On July 20, 2012, Aurora, Colorado, became the epicenter of horror when a gunman opened fire during the midnight premiere of *The Dark Knight Rises* at the Century 16 Theater. Members of the Gateway High School football team were present that evening, expecting a night of camaraderie. At 12:37 a.m., the assailant entered the theater in combat gear and opened fire, killing twelve people, injuring fifty-eight others, and traumatizing an entire city.

Within minutes, I received a call and initiated an Incident Response Team (IRT) recall—a system APS had established in 2008, shaped by lessons from Columbine. Years of tabletop and live exercises with city partners paid off. We opened Gateway High School to law enforcement as a site to interview witnesses, gather families, and provide immediate care. Other APS schools became shelters when police discovered explosives in the suspect's apartment.

As a combat fighter pilot and commander, I knew the long shadow violence casts. But as superintendent, I also understood that, while schools are not first responders, they inevitably become second, third, and even fourth responders, dealing with the psychological aftermath that touches students, families, and staff for years.

A 2013 Harvard Kennedy School case study on the Aurora theater shooting examined APS's role in detail, highlighting both the challenges and the lessons of crisis management. One of the central insights was the importance of phased recovery. On July 23—just three days after the tragedy—I laid out a three-phase recovery plan for APS. Phase One (July 20–22) addressed immediate response. Phase Two (July 23–August 6) carried the community through the reopening of schools. Phase Three (the full school year) guided long-term recovery. Segmenting the crisis in this way gave staff, students, and families confidence that we had a plan, that there was structure amid chaos. As I explained at the time: *"If you tell people a crisis will take years to overcome, they feel hopeless. But if you break it into weeks and months, they feel confident you know what you're doing."*

The Harvard Kennedy School case study also underscored seven major lessons:

1. **Impact on the Community:** The shooting left deep psychological scars on students, families, and

educators, making safety and well-being urgent imperatives.

2. **School District's Response:** APS acted quickly by opening schools, organizing community meetings, and deploying counseling services.

3. **Crisis Management and Communication:** Effective coordination with law enforcement, mental health professionals, and city partners was essential to restoring order and trust.

4. **Mental Health as a Priority:** Ongoing counseling, trauma-informed training, and supportive environments became non-negotiables in APS's recovery plan.

5. **Collaboration:** Partnerships across schools, non-profits, government agencies, and community organizations proved indispensable. APS leveraged these to enhance safety and resilience.

6. **Long-Term Resilience:** APS committed to new safety protocols, regular emergency drills, and continuous staff training to ensure preparedness.

7. **Lessons Learned:** Every crisis must serve as a catalyst for improvement. APS used the tragedy to strengthen policies, practices, and mental health resources across the district.

These findings made one point clear: Safety and security were no longer bureaucratic terms but lived imperatives. For APS, crisis management was not about policies on paper

Scribe • • • Legal

MAP

Briefing Developer

Communication

Maintenance
& Operations

Nurse

WHITEBOARD

Hazardous Control

Chief Academic
Officer

TV NEWS

Transportation

Food Services

Risk Mgmt.

Human Resources

Information
Technology

Fire Dept.

MAP

Planner • • • Police Dept.

Principal Deputy
Rep.   Supt.

COMCAST RECORDING

IRT Conference Room Layout

but about building trust, protecting students, and fostering
resilience in partnership with the wider community.

Operationally, this required discipline. Our Incident
Response Team (IRT) meetings were structured and deliberate, with every participant holding defined responsibilities
and checklists (see Appendix D, Incident Response Team
Checklists).

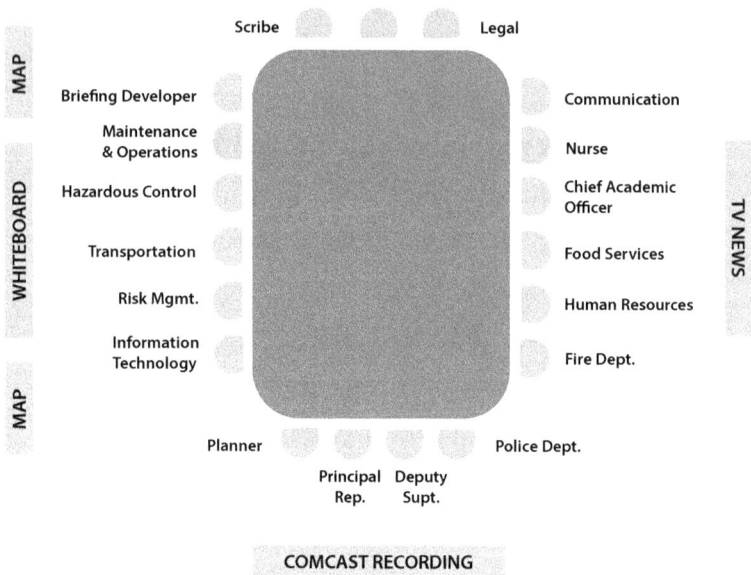

When an incident occurred, we recalled the team, established meeting times, and shared the "big picture" through
a systematic communication chain. Once assembled, we
immediately logged the facts of the crisis—who, what, where,

when, why—on whiteboards to eliminate confusion. From there, responsibilities were divided: assigning scribes to document events, dedicating separate rooms for press release drafting, establishing webinar contact with all team members, and conducting regular "hotwashes" or debriefs after every real or simulated incident to identify lessons learned and areas for improvement.

This was not theory; it was ownership in practice. By organizing, rehearsing, and refining our systems, APS demonstrated that school districts can and must prepare for crises before they occur.

The Aurora theater tragedy became a defining test of APS's ability to manage crisis through external transformation. Just as Boys & Girls Clubs and Wings Over the Rockies provided external opportunities for learning and career pathways, the partnerships forged in Aurora proved that schools also need external allies to safeguard their communities in moments of trauma. Crisis management is, in many ways, its own form of ELO—an external learning partnership between schools, law enforcement, mental health professionals, and civic organizations, all working together to protect and heal young people.

In *Super Ownership* terms, this case underscores that transformation is incomplete unless schools also own crisis preparedness. No district can stand alone. It requires foresight, partnerships, and the discipline to practice relentlessly so that when tragedy comes—as it inevitably will—students and families find schools ready not only to teach but to protect, comfort, and lead.

KEY INSIGHTS FROM CHAPTER NINE
The Urgency of Preparedness

- Crisis management should be seen as an ongoing process, not an afterthought. APS's response to the 2012 Aurora theater shooting was shaped by years of preparation through training, tabletop exercises, and coordination with local agencies like the Aurora Police Department.
- Establishing Incident Response Teams and continuously testing their readiness is critical. The importance of preparedness is echoed in the notion that school districts are "second/third/fourth responders" in the aftermath of crises.

Coordination with Local Agencies

- The collaboration between APS, law enforcement, and mental health professionals was central to the district's crisis response. This coordination ensured that resources were efficiently distributed and the needs of students, families, and staff were met swiftly and effectively.
- Forming partnerships with external agencies before a crisis is crucial. These partnerships become a lifeline

during the crisis and provide a framework for effective collaboration.

Phased Approach to Recovery

- The crisis recovery was broken down into manageable phases: immediate response (July 20–22), short-term recovery (July 23–August 6), and long-term recovery (the school year). This phased approach helped reduce the psychological burden on stakeholders and provided clarity about the steps ahead.
- A key insight here is that crisis management does not end immediately after an event; it continues long after the immediate impact, requiring consistent effort and adaptation.

Prioritizing Mental Health Support

- The focus on mental health support for all affected by the tragedy—students, staff, and families—was vital. APS implemented counseling services, provided trauma-informed training for educators, and fostered a supportive environment for healing.
- Schools must recognize their role in not just managing the logistical aspects of a crisis but also supporting the emotional and psychological needs of their community.

Crisis Communication

- Effective and clear communication during a crisis cannot be overstated. APS made it a priority to communicate frequently with the community, law enforcement, and mental health providers.
- The creation of detailed communication protocols, including the use of webinars and dedicated communication teams, ensured that key messages were delivered promptly and consistently across all channels.

Building Resilience Through Collaboration

- Building community resilience involves not only responding to the immediate crisis but also investing in long-term strategies for recovery. APS's collaborative efforts with other organizations and agencies helped to ensure that the district's recovery was supported by a broad network of resources and expertise.
- The involvement of multiple stakeholders—local government, nonprofits, and community leaders—reinforced the importance of an integrated approach to crisis management and recovery.

Learning from Experience

- Crisis situations provide invaluable learning opportunities. After the response to the Aurora theater shooting, APS engaged in a "hotwash" or debrief to assess what went well and where improvements were needed.

- Continuous reflection and revision of crisis management plans ensure that a school district can improve its readiness and responsiveness for future crises.

Operationalizing Crisis Management

- Developing a structured, operational response plan that includes team roles, checklists, and designated responsibilities is essential. The IRT should be organized ahead of time, with clear guidance on each member's role during a crisis.
- Immediate actions should include recording key events, organizing teams for specific tasks (like communication), and regularly updating all stakeholders to ensure alignment in response efforts.

The Role of School Districts in Crisis

- School districts must embrace the responsibility of managing crises by owning the process. It's not just about having a plan but also about having the systems, training, and partnerships in place to handle the complexities of crisis management before it happens.

Ongoing Commitment to Safety and Security

- Following the shooting, APS took steps to transform its approach to safety, implementing new safety protocols, conducting emergency drills, and continuously training staff.

- Safety should be embedded into the culture of the district, evolving alongside best practices and new technologies. This proactive approach helps build a sense of confidence and security within the community.

The Need for a Crisis Management Framework

- This chapter underscores the importance of having a comprehensive, actionable crisis management framework that can guide school districts through unpredictable and tragic events. It emphasizes the need for deliberate planning, ongoing exercises, and the institutionalization of crisis preparedness.
- The chapter also highlights that every school district will have unique needs and challenges but can benefit from the lessons learned through Aurora's experience.

CHAPTER QUESTIONS TO CONSIDER

1. **How prepared is your organization for a crisis of this magnitude?** Have you established an IRT, and are members of the organization regularly trained and tested?

2. **What steps have you taken to ensure effective communication during a crisis?** Do you have protocols in place for coordinating with law enforcement, mental health professionals, and community partners?

3. **How does your organization address the psychological impact of a crisis on students and staff?** What mental health support systems are currently available, and how can they be improved?

4. **In what ways can your school district build resilience to better handle future crises?** Have you considered long-term recovery plans and regular emergency drills as part of your crisis management strategy?

5. **What lessons can you draw from the Aurora Public Schools' response to the theater shooting?** How can these insights be applied to your own context to enhance crisis preparedness and response?

6. **How can your district foster collaboration with external agencies to strengthen crisis management efforts?** Are there existing partnerships that could be leveraged or new ones that should be established?

PART THREE

Putting It All Together

CHAPTER TEN

Cultivating Ownership in Transforming K-12 Education

While leadership is the cornerstone of any successful superintendency, genuine leadership isn't about racing ahead and hoping that others follow. Whether leading in the military, business, a school district, or nonprofit organizations, I have learned it is better to lead by inspiring. If all the major internal and external stakeholders have a sense of ownership for the organization, the inspiration needed is collaborative and cooperative. This makes transformations that much easier.

Ownership within the context of educational reform refers to a sense of responsibility, accountability, and investment that stakeholders (e.g., teachers, students, parents, administrators, community members) feel toward the improvement and success of the education system. It involves a mindset shift from passive participation to active engagement, where individuals take ownership of their roles and contributions in driving positive change.

Ownership in Educational Reform

In educational reform, ownership manifests in various ways:

1. **Teacher Ownership:** Teachers take ownership of their professional growth and development, actively seeking opportunities for improvement, implementing innovative teaching methods, and collaborating with colleagues to enhance student learning outcomes.

2. **Student Ownership:** Students take ownership of their learning by setting goals, monitoring their progress, and actively engaging in the learning process. They become self-directed learners who are motivated to explore, inquire, and take risks in their academic pursuits.

3. **Parent Ownership:** Parents take ownership of their children's education by actively supporting and advocating for their academic success. They engage with teachers and school administrators, participate in school activities, and provide a supportive home environment conducive to learning.

4. **Administrative Ownership:** School leaders and administrators take ownership of creating a positive school culture, fostering collaboration among staff,

and implementing policies and initiatives that promote student achievement and well-being.

5. **Community Ownership:** The broader community takes ownership of the local education system by investing resources, volunteering time and expertise, and advocating for equitable access to quality education for all students.

In essence, ownership in educational reform implies a shared commitment to collective goals, a willingness to take initiative, and a belief in the capacity of each stakeholder to contribute to the improvement of the education system. Ownership fosters a sense of pride and agency among all stakeholders, ultimately leading to more effective and sustainable reforms that positively impact student learning and success.

Ownership in education holds transformative potential in cultivating a culture characterized by accountability, collaboration, and innovation. Here's how:

Accountability:

- When individuals take ownership of their roles and responsibilities within the educational ecosystem, they inherently embrace accountability for their actions and decisions.
- Teachers who take ownership of their professional growth are more likely to hold themselves accountable

for implementing effective teaching strategies and continuously improving their instructional practices.

- Students who take ownership of their learning set high standards for themselves and hold themselves accountable for achieving their academic goals.
- Administrators who foster a culture of ownership among staff promote accountability by empowering educators to take ownership of their classrooms and fostering a sense of collective responsibility for student success.
- Ownership encourages transparency and honesty, as individuals take responsibility for their contributions and outcomes, thereby fostering a culture of trust and integrity within the educational community.

Collaboration:

- Ownership encourages collaboration among stakeholders as they work toward common goals and shared visions for educational improvement.
- Teachers who take ownership of their professional development are more likely to collaborate with colleagues, sharing best practices, resources, and expertise to enhance teaching and learning outcomes.
- Students who take ownership of their learning often engage in collaborative learning experiences, such as group projects, peer tutoring, and collaborative problem-solving, which foster a sense of teamwork and mutual support.

- Administrators who promote ownership among staff create opportunities for collaboration through Professional Learning Communities, interdisciplinary projects, and shared decision-making processes.
- Ownership fosters a culture of collective problem-solving, where stakeholders work together to address challenges, share ideas, and develop innovative solutions to improve educational practices and outcomes.

Innovation:

- Ownership empowers individuals to think creatively and take risks in pursuit of educational excellence and improvement.
- Teachers who take ownership of their classrooms are more likely to innovate by experimenting with new teaching methods, incorporating technology, and adapting instructional approaches to meet the diverse needs of their students.
- Students who take ownership of their learning are encouraged to explore their interests, pursue inquiry-based projects, and think critically and creatively about real-world problems.
- Administrators who foster ownership among staff create a supportive environment that encourages innovation, where educators feel empowered to propose new ideas, pilot innovative programs, and take calculated risks to improve student outcomes.

- Ownership stimulates a culture of continuous improvement, where stakeholders are encouraged to question existing practices, challenge the status quo, and explore new possibilities for enhancing teaching, learning, and student engagement.

- Ownership in education serves as a catalyst for accountability, collaboration, and innovation, fostering a dynamic and supportive culture that empowers stakeholders to work together toward the common goal of educational excellence, accelerating student achievement, closing achievement gaps, and being ready to deal with crisis management whenever a crisis arises.

Ownership in a Transformational Culture

Leadership plays a pivotal role in promoting a culture of ownership in education by setting the tone, modeling behavior, and providing support and resources for stakeholders to take ownership of their roles and contributions. Here's how leadership can promote ownership within educational institutions:

Setting a Mission, Vision, and Values:

- Effective leaders articulate a clear vision and core values that prioritize ownership, accountability, collaboration, and innovation in education.

- They communicate this vision and values consistently, ensuring alignment across all levels of the organization and fostering a shared sense of purpose and direction.

Modeling Ownership:

- Leaders lead by example, demonstrating ownership of their responsibilities and commitments.
- They take accountability for decisions and actions, admitting mistakes and learning from failures, which sets a precedent for others to do the same.
- By actively engaging in professional development, reflecting on their practice, and seeking feedback, leaders model a commitment to continuous improvement and lifelong learning.

EMPOWERING STAKEHOLDERS:

- Leaders empower teachers, students, parents, staff, and community organizations (e.g., Parent-Teacher Organizations, Community Workforce Committees) to take ownership of their respective roles and contributions.
- Leaders delegate authority and decision-making responsibilities, giving individuals autonomy and agency to make meaningful contributions to the educational process.
- When superintendents provide opportunities for professional growth, leadership development, and shared management, they cultivate a culture where everyone

feels valued and empowered to contribute to the collective goals of the organization.

- Superintendents strengthen partnerships with the community to create a sense of shared ownership and use technology as a tool for fostering ownership and collaboration (webinars, podcasts, electronic recurring letters).

CREATING A SUPPORTIVE ENVIRONMENT:

- Leaders create a supportive environment where risk-taking, experimentation, and innovation are encouraged and celebrated.
- They provide resources, time, and professional learning opportunities to support stakeholders in their efforts to innovate and improve educational practices.
- By fostering a culture of trust, collaboration, and open communication, leaders create a safe space where individuals feel comfortable taking ownership of their ideas, initiatives, and challenges.

RECOGNIZING AND CELEBRATING SUCCESS:

- Leaders recognize and celebrate achievements, both big and small, that demonstrate ownership, collaboration, and innovation.
- Leaders acknowledge the efforts and contributions of stakeholders, highlighting examples of ownership in

action and showcasing the positive impact it has on student learning and school culture.

- By celebrating successes publicly and sharing best practices, leaders inspire others to embrace ownership and strive for excellence in their own work.

PROVIDING FEEDBACK AND SUPPORT:

- Leaders provide constructive feedback and support to help stakeholders develop their ownership mindset and skills.
- They offer guidance, mentorship, and coaching to individuals as they navigate challenges, pursue professional growth opportunities, and implement innovative practices.
- By fostering a culture of continuous improvement and learning, leaders encourage stakeholders to reflect on their experiences, learn from feedback, and adapt their approaches to better meet the needs of students and the community.

In essence, leadership plays a critical role in promoting a culture of ownership in education by fostering a supportive environment, empowering stakeholders, and modeling the behaviors and values that are conducive to ownership, collaboration, and innovation. Through effective leadership, educational institutions can cultivate a culture where everyone feels a sense of ownership and responsibility for the success of students and the overall improvement of the education system.

Ownership with Measurement

Measuring the impact of ownership on academic performance, student engagement, and overall school culture involves a combination of qualitative and quantitative assessment methods. Here are some approaches to consider:

Surveys and Interviews

Conduct surveys and interviews with teachers, students, parents, and staff to gather qualitative data on their perceptions of ownership within the school community. Gathering stakeholder voices through structured surveys and in-depth interviews is critical to understanding the culture of ownership at every level of the educational ecosystem. These tools not only provide valuable data but also signal to the community that their perspectives are valued in the district's continuous improvement process. Surveys can be designed to reach broad audiences and uncover patterns, while interviews allow for more personal, nuanced reflections. Together, they provide a balanced picture of how ownership is experienced and perceived across the system.

Ask questions about their sense of responsibility, empowerment, and collaboration and their attitudes toward teaching, learning, and school culture. To assess the presence and depth of ownership, inquiry must go beyond surface-level satisfaction. Key themes to explore include: "Do you feel personally responsible for student success?" "Do you believe your ideas are heard and valued?" "How often do you collaborate with others to improve outcomes?" and "How would you describe your school's learning culture?" These questions reveal how empowered individuals feel, how aligned they are with shared goals, and whether collaboration is seen as a norm or a burden. Analyzing this data helps identify strongholds of ownership and areas needing strategic attention.

Use open-ended questions to capture detailed insights, anecdotes, and examples of how ownership has influenced their experiences and outcomes. Open-ended questions invite stories—rich, authentic narratives that often reveal more than any data point can. These can be prompts such as, "Describe a time when you took initiative to improve something in your classroom or school," or "What does taking ownership mean to you?" Allow stakeholders to share personal examples of responsibility, innovation, and commitment. These insights can shed light on what drives motivation, where barriers exist, and how leadership can further cultivate a climate of shared ownership. When compiled and shared, these testimonials become a powerful tool for inspiration, reflection, and continuous improvement across the district.

Share testimonials and success stories from stakeholders who have embraced ownership, including teachers who redesigned classroom instruction to meet student needs, principals who led turnaround efforts in underperforming schools, students who took charge of their learning through goal-setting and reflection, and community partners who collaborated to expand access to real-world learning opportunities. These stories humanize the impact of ownership and serve as powerful evidence that when individuals at every level take responsibility for outcomes, sustainable transformation becomes possible. Collecting and highlighting these narratives reinforces a culture where ownership is celebrated, expected, and continuously cultivated.

Observations:

- Conduct classroom observations to assess the extent to which teachers and students demonstrate ownership in their teaching and learning practices.
- Look for and celebrate evidence of student autonomy, initiative, and engagement, as well as teacher responsiveness, adaptability, and innovation.
- Use observation protocols or rubrics to systematically document observations and identify patterns or trends related to ownership behaviors and practices.

Academic Performance Data:

- Analyze academic performance data, such as standardized test scores, course grades, and graduation rates, to assess the impact of ownership on student achievement.

- Compare performance trends over time and across different student populations to identify correlations between ownership practices and academic outcomes.
- Consider disaggregating data by demographic variables (e.g., race, ethnicity, socioeconomic status) to ensure equitable outcomes for all students.

Attendance and Dropout Rates:

- Examine attendance and dropout rates to gauge the impact of ownership on student engagement and retention.
- Compare attendance and dropout rates before and after implementing ownership initiatives to assess changes in student behavior and motivation.

Discipline and Behavior Incidents:

- Monitor discipline referrals, suspensions, and other behavior incidents to evaluate the influence of ownership on school culture and climate.
- Look for reductions in disciplinary actions and improvements in student conduct, respect, and responsibility.

Parent and Community Involvement

Assess levels of parent and community involvement in school activities, events, and decision-making processes to measure the impact of ownership on school-community partnerships. Ownership in education extends beyond the walls of the classroom. True transformation requires authentic partnerships between schools, families, and the broader community. Assessing parent and community involvement helps reveal the extent to which stakeholders feel invited, empowered, and responsible for student success. This includes not only participation in visible events but also engagement in strategic conversations, advocacy efforts, and shared accountability for outcomes. A high level of involvement often signals a strong sense of ownership—when parents see themselves as co-educators, and community partners view schools as integral to civic and economic vitality.

Track participation rates in parent-teacher conferences, school events, volunteer programs, and advisory committees. Quantitative data such as attendance at parent-teacher conferences, open houses, family literacy nights, and athletic or arts events can serve as an early indicator of engagement. But meaningful ownership is further reflected in more sustained and strategic forms of involvement—such as parent representation on school improvement teams, advisory boards, or curriculum review committees. Volunteer hours logged, community mentorship programs launched, and partnerships formed with local businesses or nonprofit organizations offer additional layers of insight into how deeply the community is invested in the educational mission. Trends in this data can identify where efforts are succeeding and where additional outreach or inclusion strategies may be necessary.

Beyond raw participation rates, it is essential to understand why parents and community members engage—or why they don't. Focus groups, surveys, or informal listening sessions can identify the conditions that encourage or inhibit meaningful involvement. Are parents informed and welcomed into decision-making, or do they feel their contributions are symbolic rather than impactful? Are community partners aligned with school goals, or do they need clearer pathways for collaboration? Understanding these dynamics can help school leaders refine engagement strategies and better support a culture where shared ownership becomes the norm.

Celebrate and communicate shared wins. Highlighting examples where community and parent involvement has led to improved outcomes—whether it's a jointly sponsored student internship program, a successful school safety initiative, or a family-led literacy campaign—reinforces the message that everyone has a role in educational success. Sharing these stories in newsletters, on websites, or at public events helps build momentum, fosters pride, and models what ownership looks like in action.

Qualitative Case Studies:

- Conduct in-depth case studies of individual classrooms, schools, or districts to explore the nuanced impact of ownership on academic performance, student engagement, and school culture.

- Use a mix of interviews, observations, document analysis, and artifact collection to capture rich, context-specific insights into the dynamics of ownership within the educational context.

Longitudinal Studies:

- Conduct longitudinal studies to track the long-term impact of ownership initiatives on academic performance, student engagement, and school culture over multiple years.
- Follow cohorts of students and stakeholders over time to assess changes in outcomes and identify factors contributing to sustained improvements in ownership practices and outcomes.
- By employing a variety of assessment methods, educational leaders can gain a comprehensive understanding of the impact of ownership on academic performance, student engagement, and overall school culture, enabling them to make informed decisions and drive continuous improvement efforts.

Sustaining the Momentum of Ownership

Sustaining a culture of ownership beyond the initial phase of transformation in a K-12 school district requires deliberate and ongoing efforts to embed ownership principles into the fabric of the organization. Here are some strategies to consider:

Leadership Continuity and Commitment:
Leadership continuity and commitment is important. Broad Center analysis shows that most big-district superintendents stay in their role more than six years and that three to five years are necessary for a superintendent to achieve momentum in their initiatives.

- Ensure continuity in leadership by nurturing a pipeline of leaders who understand and champion the values of ownership.
- Maintain a strong commitment from school and district leaders to prioritize ownership as a core value and incorporate it into strategic planning and decision-making processes.

Professional Development and Capacity Building:

- Provide ongoing professional development opportunities for teachers, administrators, and staff to deepen their understanding of ownership principles and develop the skills necessary to foster ownership in others.
- Offer workshops, seminars, coaching, and mentorship programs focused on topics such as leadership, collaboration, innovation, and continuous improvement.

Embed Ownership in Policies and Practices:

- Embed ownership principles into school policies, procedures, and practices to institutionalize a culture of ownership.

- Ensure that hiring, evaluation, and recognition systems reward individuals who demonstrate ownership behaviors and contribute to a positive school culture.
- Integrate ownership into curriculum development, instructional practices, and assessment strategies to promote student ownership of learning.

Promote Distributed Leadership and Shared Decision-Making:

- Foster distributed leadership by empowering teachers, students, parents, and community members to take on leadership roles and participate in shared decision-making processes.
- Establish structures, such as school leadership teams, committees, and advisory boards, to facilitate collaboration and input from diverse stakeholders in school governance and decision-making.

Continuous Communication and Feedback:

- Maintain open and transparent communication channels to keep stakeholders informed about the progress of ownership initiatives and solicit feedback on their effectiveness.
- Regularly communicate the vision, values, and expectations related to ownership through newsletters, meetings, and other communication platforms.
- Collect and analyze feedback from stakeholders through surveys, focus groups, and informal

conversations to identify areas for improvement and adaptation.

Celebrate and Reinforce Successes:

- Celebrate and recognize individuals and teams who exemplify ownership behaviors and contribute to a positive school culture.
- Share success stories, best practices, and lessons learned through newsletters, staff meetings, and professional development sessions to inspire and motivate others.
- Create rituals and traditions that reinforce a sense of pride, ownership, and belonging within the school community.

Adapt and Evolve:

- Continuously monitor and assess the cultural climate and dynamics within the school district to identify emerging challenges and opportunities.
- Be flexible and adaptive in responding to changing needs and circumstances, adjusting strategies and initiatives as necessary to sustain a culture of ownership.
- Encourage experimentation, innovation, and continuous improvement by fostering a culture of learning, reflection, and adaptation.

By implementing these strategies, K-12 school districts can create a sustainable culture of ownership that empowers stakeholders, fosters collaboration, and drives continuous improvement in student outcomes and school performance.

Looking Ahead

Cultivating ownership in K-12 education has profound implications for the future of learning, shaping not only how students engage with educational content but also their development as lifelong learners and active participants in society. Here are some broader implications to consider:

Empowerment and Agency:

- Cultivating ownership empowers students to take control of their learning journey, fostering a sense of agency and self-efficacy with project based learning where student pick a project, work as a team, and out-brief as a team all while meeting state standards.
- By giving students opportunities to make choices, set goals, and pursue their interests, ownership promotes a deeper sense of engagement and investment in learning. Choice is ownership, ownership is motivation, and motivation is success.

Personalized Learning:

- Ownership supports the shift toward personalized learning, where instruction is tailored to meet the individual needs, interests, and learning styles of each student. Teachers work with pacing guides to ensure all criteria for a semester is covered but with the flexibility to meet the various needs of their students.

- By allowing students to take ownership of their learning pathways and pace, educators can better meet students where they are and provide more relevant and meaningful learning experiences.

Critical Thinking and Problem-Solving:

- Ownership encourages students to think critically, solve problems, and take initiative in exploring complex issues and finding creative solutions.
- By engaging students as active participants in the learning process, ownership promotes higher order thinking skills such as analysis, evaluation, and synthesis.

Twenty-First-Century Skills:

- Ownership fosters the development of twenty-first-century skills such as communication, collaboration, creativity, and resilience.
- By working collaboratively on projects, taking risks, and reflecting on their experiences, students develop the skills and dispositions necessary to thrive in an ever-changing global landscape.
- Foster concurrent enrollment in which high schools partner with community colleges in allowing teachers with master's degrees to work as adjunct professors so

students have opportunities to earn college credit in high school.

Preparation for Citizenship and Civic Engagement:

* Ownership prepares students to become informed and engaged citizens who actively participate in their communities and contribute to the common good.
* By fostering a sense of responsibility, empathy, and social awareness, ownership equips students with the skills and mindset needed to address real-world challenges and advocate for positive change.

Lifelong Learning and Adaptability:

* Ownership instills a love of learning and a growth mindset, encouraging students to embrace challenges, learn from failure, and persist in the face of obstacles.
* By cultivating a culture of curiosity, exploration, and continuous improvement, ownership prepares students to adapt to new technologies, industries, and societal changes throughout their lives.

Equity and Inclusion:

* Ownership promotes equity and inclusion by recognizing and valuing the diverse backgrounds, perspectives, and experiences of all students.
* By creating opportunities for voice and choice, ownership ensures that students from diverse backgrounds

can see themselves reflected in the curriculum and their voices are heard in the learning process.

In summary, cultivating ownership in K-12 education has far-reaching implications for the future of learning, empowering students to become active agents in their own education and preparing them to thrive in a rapidly changing world. By prioritizing ownership, educators can create learning environments that inspire curiosity, foster creativity, and equip students with the skills and dispositions they need to succeed in the twenty-first century and beyond.

Next are some of the results of using the insights in this book that were applied at Aurora Public Schools (APS) over seven years.

Evidence of Internal and External Transformation Success

From 2006 to 2013, APS underwent a transformation that not only reversed years of stagnation but set a precedent for K-12 innovation nationwide. The district's leadership focused on measurable outcomes, accountability, and strategic partnerships, resulting in significant gains across multiple domains. These achievements became a national model, underscored by the expansion of APS's concurrent enrollment program to a statewide initiative under Governor Bill Ritter and later to a national level.

GRADUATION RATE IMPROVEMENT

Before 2006, APS's graduation rates fell behind state averages, with pronounced disparities among minority and low-income students. Recognizing the urgency of the situation, the district implemented a series of data-driven interventions. The On-Track Indicator System monitored attendance, grades, and behavior, allowing educators to identify and support at-risk students before they fell too far behind. Credit recovery programs expanded online learning, summer school access, and flexible scheduling options, ensuring that students who had previously struggled had viable pathways to graduation.

A critical component of this success was the district's emphasis on postsecondary readiness. By forging partnerships with local colleges, trade schools, and employers, APS integrated career training, dual enrollment, and internship opportunities into the high school experience. As a result, graduation rates rose by double-digit percentage points, with APS outperforming state averages in improving outcomes for underserved populations.

Impact: APS significantly improved its graduation rate, reversing years of stagnation.

- **Before 2006:** Graduation rates were below state averages, with significant disparities among student demographics.
- **By 2013:** Graduation rates had risen notably, particularly among historically underserved populations.

Key Initiatives:

- **On-Track Indicator System:** Implemented early warning systems to track attendance, grades, and behavior. Used data-driven interventions to support struggling students before they fell off track.
- **Credit Recovery Programs:** Expanded access to online learning and summer school programs for students needing additional credits. Increased flexible learning opportunities, including evening and weekend programs.
- **Postsecondary and Workforce Readiness Alignment:** Partnered with local colleges and trade schools to provide career and technical training. Implemented dual enrollment programs so students could earn college credit in high school. Strengthened partnerships with local employers, increasing internships and real-world learning experiences.

Measured Results:

- Graduation rates increased by double-digit percentage points.
- APS exceeded state improvement averages in graduation rates for minority and low-income students.

LITERACY GAINS AND ACADEMIC PERFORMANCE

APS made early literacy a cornerstone of its academic reforms. The district implemented a K-3 literacy emphasis, using reading benchmarks to assess students multiple times per year. Those falling behind received intensive intervention, while teachers benefited from enhanced professional development in literacy instruction. The curriculum shifted from a standardized approach to one that emphasized differentiated instruction tailored to individual student needs.

Further innovations included the introduction of literacy block schedules and expanded writing components across all subjects, reinforcing reading comprehension. Technology played a pivotal role, with adaptive learning software and 1:1 device initiatives enabling personalized instruction at home and in the classroom. These efforts produced measurable results, with a notable increase in the percentage of students reading at grade level by third grade and improved state assessment scores in literacy across multiple grade levels.

Impact: Improved student performance in literacy, particularly in early grades, leading to long-term academic success.

Key Initiatives:

- **K-3 Literacy Emphasis (Early Intervention Model):** Used reading benchmarks to assess students multiple times per year. Introduced intensive reading intervention for students below grade level. Expanded professional development for teachers in literacy instruction.

- **Strategic Curriculum Overhaul:** Shifted from a standardized approach to *differentiated instruction* based on student needs. Implemented literacy block schedules to ensure dedicated time for reading. Strengthened writing components across all subjects to reinforce literacy skills.
- **Technology Integration in Literacy Learning:** Expanded access to adaptive learning software tailored to student reading levels. Piloted 1:1 device programs to supplement literacy instruction at home.

Measured Results:

- Increased percentage of students reading at grade level by third grade.
- Improved state assessment scores in literacy across multiple grade levels.

TRUANCY REDUCTION AND ATTENDANCE GAINS

Chronic absenteeism and truancy posed significant challenges for APS students before 2006. To combat this, the district established a Truancy Task Force, bringing together educators, social workers, and community liaisons to identify and address the root causes of absenteeism. By increasing school-based support and family engagement initiatives, APS fostered a culture of accountability and attendance.

Restorative justice programs replaced punitive disciplinary measures with intervention-focused approaches, offering students mentorship and community connections instead of suspensions. Flexible learning models, including alternative education centers and blended learning options, provided pathways for students who struggled in traditional settings. These initiatives led to a significant drop in truancy rates and increased attendance across all grade levels. In addition, suspension rates decreased, reflecting a broader shift toward intervention over discipline.

Key Initiatives:

- **Truancy Task Force and Family Engagement:** Created school-based intervention teams working with families to address root causes of absenteeism. Increased access to school-based social workers and community liaisons.
- **Restorative Justice Programs:** Shifted from punitive disciplinary measures (suspensions) to intervention-based approaches. Implemented mentorship programs pairing students with community leaders and older peers.
- **Alternative and Flexible Learning Models:** Opened alternative education centers for students who struggled in traditional settings. Implemented *blended learning options,* allowing students to recover credits online.

Measured Results:

- Truancy rates dropped significantly, with attendance rates improving across all grade levels.
- Suspension rates decreased, indicating a shift toward intervention over discipline.

WORKFORCE AND POSTSECONDARY READINESS

The transformation of APS extended beyond K-12 education, as the district became a leader in preparing students for college and the workforce. Career pathway programs in high-demand industries such as aerospace, healthcare, and STEM provided students with real-world experience through internships, job shadowing, and mentorship programs.

One of the district's most groundbreaking achievements was its concurrent enrollment expansion. Initially piloted in APS, this program enabled students to earn high school and college credit in their respective high school building taught by high school teachers who were also adjunct professors of the Community College of Aurora. This innovative program effectively reduced financial and time barriers to higher education. Under Governor Bill Ritter, the initiative was adopted statewide, ultimately influencing national policy. This concurrent enrollment program was recognized on a national stage when Linda Bowman, president of the Community College of Aurora, and I were interviewed on the CNN program *Fareed Zakaria GPS* on December 14, 2014.

Additional efforts to improve postsecondary outcomes included increased Free Application for Federal Student Aid (FAFSA) completion rates through targeted workshops and expanded college and career counseling for first-generation college students. These initiatives resulted in a substantial increase in APS graduates enrolling in postsecondary education, with many completing industry certifications before graduation.

Key Initiatives:

- **Career Pathways Programs:** Established sector-specific career tracks in industries such as aerospace, healthcare, and STEM. Partnered with local businesses for internships, job shadowing, and mentorship programs.
- **Concurrent Enrollment Expansion:** Strengthened partnerships with local community colleges and universities. Created early college programs allowing students to graduate from high school with an associate's degree.
- **Increased Access to FAFSA and College Counseling:** Implemented workshops to increase FAFSA completion rates. Expanded college and career counseling, particularly for first-generation college students.

Measured Results:

- Increased percentage of APS graduates enrolling in postsecondary education.
- Significant growth in students completing industry certifications before graduation.

COMMUNITY ENGAGEMENT AND EXTERNAL PARTNERSHIPS

APS's shift from an internally focused district to a community-centered institution was instrumental in its success. The Community Workforce Planning Team (CWPT) brought together educators, business leaders, and local stakeholders to align educational offerings with workforce demands. Career exploration programs introduced middle school students to potential career paths, ensuring early exposure to future opportunities.

Parent engagement saw a significant boost through enhanced bilingual outreach, parent academies, and dedicated community liaisons. Public-private partnerships flourished, with aerospace organizations, healthcare institutions, and technology companies investing in APS students through mentorship programs and funding initiatives. These efforts resulted in increased parent participation in school events and a growing network of businesses actively supporting student development.

Impact: APS successfully transitioned from an internally focused district to one that engaged community organizations, businesses, and higher education to support student success.

Key Initiatives:

- **Community Workforce Planning Team:** Brought together educators, business leaders, and community stakeholders to align education with workforce needs. Established career exploration opportunities for students as early as middle school.
- **Parent and Family Engagement Programs:** Increased communication strategies, including bilingual outreach and parent academies. Developed community liaisons to connect families to school and social services.
- **Public-Private Partnerships:** Strengthened collaborations with aerospace organizations, healthcare institutions, and tech companies. Expanded community-based after-school programs in partnership with nonprofits.

Measured Results:

- Increased parent engagement, as measured by participation in school events and feedback surveys.
- More businesses and organizations actively invested in APS students through mentorship and funding programs.

INFRASTRUCTURE AND TECHNOLOGY ENHANCEMENTS

Recognizing that modern learning environments are critical to student success, APS made substantial investments in its infrastructure. Renovations to aging school buildings, along with the construction of new facilities, ensured that students had access to cutting-edge educational spaces. Expanded STEM labs, technology centers, and vocational training facilities enabled hands-on learning experiences aligned with industry needs.

Technology integration further transformed instruction, with APS expanding its 1:1 device initiative to ensure every student had access to a tablet or laptop. Adaptive learning platforms facilitated personalized instruction in key subjects such as math and reading. To address the digital divide, the district partnered with local governments and private providers to increase internet access for low-income families, while digital literacy programs equipped both students and parents with essential technology skills.

Impact: APS invested in modernizing learning environments to ensure students had access to cutting-edge technology and safe, innovative school spaces.

Key Initiatives:

- **Facility Upgrades and New School Construction:** Renovated aging schools and built new facilities to meet growing enrollment demands. Expanded

STEM labs, technology centers, and vocational training spaces.

- **Technology Integration for Personalized Learning:** Expanded the district's 1:1 student device initiative (tablets/laptops for all students). Implemented adaptive learning platforms, improving personalized instruction in math and reading.
- **Expanded Wi-Fi and Digital Equity Initiatives:** Partnered with local government and private providers to increase internet access for low-income families. Developed digital literacy programs for both students and parents.

Measured Results:

- Improved student engagement in digital learning platforms.
- Increased use of classroom technology to support individualized instruction.

Between 2006 and 2013, APS emerged as a national leader in educational innovation, achieving measurable gains in graduation rates, literacy, attendance, workforce readiness, community engagement, and infrastructure development. The district's pioneering efforts in concurrent enrollment set a precedent for education policy nationwide, earning national recognition on Fareed Zakaria's GPS show in 2024.

APS's transformation was not the result of a single program or initiative but rather a comprehensive approach centered on data-driven decision-making, strategic partnerships, and an unwavering commitment to student success. The lessons learned from this period serve as a blueprint for districts seeking to improve outcomes and prepare students for the challenges of the twenty-first century.

CHAPTER QUESTIONS TO CONSIDER

1. **Reflecting on Your Role:** How do you currently see your role in fostering ownership within your educational community? What steps can you take to enhance this sense of ownership among your stakeholders?

2. **Challenges and Opportunities:** What challenges have you encountered when trying to cultivate ownership in your educational environment? How might you overcome these obstacles to create a more collaborative and accountable culture?

3. **Leadership in Action:** As a leader or educator, how can you model the behaviors that promote ownership and inspire others to take responsibility for their roles in the education system?

4. **Sustaining Ownership:** What strategies can you implement to ensure that the culture of ownership remains strong and continues to grow over time, even as leadership or circumstances change?

5. **Measuring Success:** How will you measure the impact of ownership on student outcomes, teacher effectiveness, and overall school culture? What metrics or indicators will be most meaningful in your context?

6. **Community Engagement:** How can you involve parents and the broader community in the ownership of your school's mission and goals? What partnerships or initiatives could strengthen this sense of shared responsibility?

7. **Personalized Learning:** In what ways can ownership be used to personalize learning for students in your school or district? How might this approach enhance student engagement and achievement?

8. **Equity and Inclusion:** How can fostering ownership help address issues of equity and inclusion in your school? What steps can you take to ensure that all students feel empowered to take control of their learning journey?

CHAPTER ELEVEN

Modeling Leadership

Over these many years, in my many leadership positions, I have found it useful to provide a "Modeling Lecture for Leadership" so potential supervisors can learn to build their own story on how they operate in a supervisory position. My basic premise is that every leader needs to develop a leadership model that they can pass on from their own experiences to future generations. A key responsibility of any leader in any profession is to prepare the next level of leadership.

This does not presuppose that what I am about to cover is the end all and be all of leadership. It is, however, *a way*, not *the way* on how one might approach this effort and the reader should take what they need to fill their own "leadership bucket" and be able to explain to their team or future teams how they operate. I always say, if you take 60 percent of what is offered here and fill the rest with your own style, this reading will have served its purpose.

What I have found useful in this regard is to model leadership by telling stories. While there are many leadership theories and books that are amazing renditions of what leadership is and can be, I have found it useful to relate stories and insights. Most people don't memorize data and theories, but they do remember examples of life experiences, good or bad, that they can embrace, reject, or adapt.

The following stories aren't always about educational issues. In the military, I would study business, health, and the arts to see how leadership was effective in other disciplines and try to apply them, when useful, to my world at the time. When I was superintendent, I would read and reflect on my experiences in the military or relate my lessons in business to see what insights might be applicable. Since I have left education, I have used stories I embraced for leadership while a superintendent to other disciplines.

Fresh Perspectives

To begin with I have always asked new supervisors who worked for me to visit in my office for an introduction to the history, funding, successes, and challenges we were facing at the time. Yes, this was factual data on the new organization to give them some keen knowledge of the team they were joining.

But at the end of the meeting, I would give them "homework." What I would say is there is a "rock in the road" that I step over out of habit and no longer see. They, on the other hand, were looking at our organization with a fresh set of eyes. My challenge was to come back in six weeks with a list of things that they liked, things they found troubling, and any new programs that they had in their previous job that could be useful for their new teammates. These comments and suggestions weren't restricted to their specific discipline. It could be comments on the HR process, the cleanliness of the facilities, or the meeting structures. Anything, really. I would also tell them that their fresh set of eyes were time limited, because after a while they won't be able to see those rocks in the road anymore, either. I always found it rewarding to see what a new supervisor would come up with once I gave them permission to observe and report on conditions in the organization.

A Tone of Confidence, Competence, and Behavior

Never underestimate the influence a leader has on an organization. I have learned that a new leader can have an almost immediate effect on staff, a school, and a school district. A new leader of an organization, especially an organization that you are trying to transform, can have an impact over a very short time. However, one must be very careful regarding how this is done, taking time for a ninety-day listening tour before you start changing things—except regarding safety or discipline issues that might require some immediate action.

When I was in the Air Force, I got pretty good at visiting squadrons and quickly picking up the leadership style of the commander. When I was a superintendent, I could apply this insight to understanding how school principals were operating within a visit or two. I saw how much the leader set the organizational environment, regarding confidence, competence, and behavior.

If a principal was a consistent micro-manager or a hands-off person, it was evident quickly. If the leader was charismatic or stern in their approach, it was evident quickly. I'm not saying any one of these is better than another; leadership can take many forms depending on the situation. But it is interesting how one person at the top of the school or district can have an impact on the entire organization.

In understanding the impact that a leader has on the environment, one must also realize that a leader lives in a "glass house." If you ever think that no will notice your mistake and you can get away with it, you are sorely mistaken. Your approach to being a leader must come with an understanding that your actions and behavior reflect greatly on your subordinates and there cannot be two ways of dealing with your way of acting and others. You set the example.

I was a Wing Commander in Turkey when I took a shortcut and crossed a security line because I was in a hurry. This was way off the beaten path, and no one was around. Within an hour, my immediate staff got calls on how the boss had broken the rules. Even while you're off duty or on vacation, don't suppose for a minute that since you are out of sight and out of mind, your poor behavior will not get back to your team. There's no need to be paranoid. But always be aware that as a leader your behavior reflects on your district.

What Kind of Leader Are You?

I have been asked many times what kind of leader I am. Do I micro-manage? Do I operate hands off? Do I lead with charisma?

It depends!

Let me describe it this way. Think of levers for every principal that you have in the school district as a superintendent. I will demonstrate this using time as a median of explanation to help demonstrate the point but not something I necessarily would do. If there is a new principal, I would have the lever full forward and have them check in with me daily. For a principal who has been in charge for a while, I would have the lever back a bit and ask them to check in with me weekly. For a principal who has demonstrated excellence over a long period of time, I would have the lever way back and ask them to check in with me monthly. I may move the lever forward even for a principal where I have had the lever way back because something may have changed in their lives, like a spouse or child is sick. In this case I would move the lever forward for a while and then probably move it back once the experienced principal has resolved the issue or had to time to recover. So, it depends! And you need to be nimble on how you lead at any given time.

I am not a believer in micro-management as a consistent tool for a leader. However, I am a believer in micro-information. In my case, one of the ways to keep a boss from micro-managing is to keep them informed so they are not surprised. If you as a subordinate are asking whether you should inform your leader about a concerning issue, then you have already crossed the line and it is better to communicate. My general rule is, "If there is a doubt, there is no doubt."

Understanding the Rhythm of an Organization

Every organization has a rhythm—a pace, flow, or pattern in how it operates day to day. This rhythm includes how people interact, how decisions are made, how processes unfold, and how the organization responds to change. Leaders must learn to sense and adjust to this rhythm. It's not something you can find in a manual; you feel it. You see it in the energy of a staff meeting, the cadence of decision-making, the responsiveness of teams, and the consistency of daily operations.

Rhythm can be disrupted—and not always for negative reasons. Moving into a new school building, renovating office space, implementing a new student information system, or changing the bell schedule can all temporarily throw off the rhythm. But the organization usually finds its way back to normal after the adjustment period. More significantly, the rhythm shifts when a new leader arrives. Different leadership styles, expectations, communication habits, and decision-making processes alter how the organization flows. That's not necessarily bad; it's just a reality that leaders and teams must recognize and work through.

However, rhythm can also unravel for the wrong reasons—when systems are overloaded, communication breaks down, or when pressure is applied too quickly without regard for capacity.

Let me share a story from my time as a commander of an F-16 fighter squadron in Utah that illustrates what it means to lead through a disruption in rhythm.

We had experienced a long stretch of poor winter weather, which meant we had to cancel a lot of our scheduled flights. To maintain pilot proficiency and meet training requirements, we planned a "surge"—a few intensive days of flying designed to catch up on lost flight hours.

Normally, our squadron operated on a two-wave flight schedule per day. For example, we might launch twelve aircraft in the morning, then another eight in the afternoon. That pace kept operations safe, predictable, and manageable. But during this surge, we were directed to fly four waves in a single day: the first wave would launch twelve aircraft, the second wave ten, the third wave eight, and the final wave six. Internally, we referred to that as a "twelve-turn-ten-turn-eight-turn-six" day. Each "turn" referred to a new group of aircraft launching after the previous group returned, refueled, and underwent basic maintenance checks.

I had to attend a meeting at the start of the day and wasn't present for the first launch. When I returned to the squadron, the second wave was just taking off. I immediately sensed something was off. The first wave had been riddled with cancellations—aircraft that couldn't fly due to maintenance issues or pilots who were sick. And as the second wave began landing, I was informed that eight out of ten aircraft had returned with in-flight emergencies—everything from mechanical problems to warning lights that forced pilots to cut missions short.

To make matters worse, while preparing the third wave, one of my most experienced instructor pilots accidentally flipped the wrong switch during engine start. This released toxic hydrazine gas—a dangerous substance used to power the emergency system in the F-16—which triggered an evacuation of the entire flight line.

At that point, the rhythm was completely broken. The team was stressed, the aircraft were unreliable, and we were losing focus. I made the call to cancel the rest of the day's flying. Within minutes, my boss—the Wing Commander—called to ask what was going on. I explained the situation in clear terms: "Sir, the rhythm is shot. We're pushing too hard. If we keep going like this, we're going to break something—or someone."

He listened, understood, and backed me up. We regrouped. The maintainers got to work fixing the jets, and the pilots recalibrated their flight plans. The next day, we flew thirty-six successful sorties with just one minor deviation. The difference? We got the rhythm back.

When you sense that the rhythm of your organization is slipping—whether due to stress, miscommunication, overload, or misalignment—it's your responsibility as a leader to step in and reset. Sometimes that means slowing things down. Sometimes it means pressing pause altogether. Because if the rhythm collapses, performance and safety follow close behind.

Recognizing and respecting the rhythm of your organization—especially during times of high demand or transition—is not a soft skill. It's a leadership imperative.

Honesty, Integrity, and Loyalty

This is a story about disciplining a member of your team. There were two Air Force Academy graduates who were from the same class and best of friends. They went to pilot training together, and they dated women who became best friends. Over the years both couples had children who were best of friends. Years later they were assigned together in the same squadron. Both had proven to be highly qualified fighter pilots, but one was made a flight commander and the other assistant flight commander— like if one was a principal and the other one was an assistant principal.

One day the assistant flight commander was flying and violated several rules of engagement on a training mission; he flew too low, too close to other aircraft, and too fast. As flight commander, his best friend called him on it and grounded him. If you ever must discipline someone who is quite a bit lower in the organization and you don't know them very well, it isn't very difficult to call them in and pick an appropriate correction. But disciplining someone who is close to you personally and a good friend is tough.

The assistant flight commander asked his best friend to give him a break, but the flight commander kept the grounding correction. The two friends didn't talk to each other for weeks. Finally, the disciplined assistant flight commander went into his best friend's office, owned up to his actions, and said that the grounding had been appropriate for the betterment of the team. That took courage. The flight commander passed the test on honesty, integrity, and loyalty. The assistant flight commander, although it took a while, also finally passed the test of honesty, integrity, and loyalty.

Three Kinds of People in the World

As a follow-on to the story above, here is a generalization that helps in understanding that there are three kinds of people in the world. Generalizations can be dangerous, but I hope to demonstrate some significant points that may help.

An Admiral once told me the story that he would explain to promising officers that there are three kinds of people in the world: the improvers, the storekeepers, and the degraders. Improvers are people who go above and beyond and leave any task better than they found it. Storekeepers do only what they are asked to do, but they do it well; they are incredibly valuable to keep any organization running. Degraders come in two categories: they do things wrong out of omission or commission.

When someone does something wrong out of omission, the decision to discipline is easier because they knew it was wrong and they did it anyway. Some examples would be breaking the law regarding drugs or touching a child inappropriately. A person who does something wrong out of omission, however, made a mistake and may need training or a corrective action that can be remedied. With omission situations where the employee wants to learn and improve, don't be a one-mistake organization.

Storekeepers and improvers can be described in a story from this Admiral friend of mine. He once had a logistics problem on his ship that needed to be resolved. He called in two junior officers separately and gave them the same task, without them knowing about it. The first officer came back with the problem solved, and he did exactly what he was asked to do; this is a storekeeper. The second officer came back with the problem solved, but he also recommended a revision to the policy that pertained to the challenge, recommended a personnel addition to make sure the problem wouldn't occur again, and had a list of three potential candidates for consideration.

We want degraders who do things wrong out of omission to elevate to the storekeeper level, and we want storekeepers to elevate to the improver level. This takes leadership and a conscious effort to know your people.

Watch Your Best Person Carefully

Communicate clearly that asking for help is a measure of strength, not a measure of weakness. I learned that when a person was elevated to a true leadership position, they needed to be reminded of this. Why? Many new persons of talent who are elevated to a position of leadership want to convince their leaders that they know what they're doing and they feel that if they ask for help they are showing weakness. The truth is, when you take on a new leadership position, you will do things for the first time and won't always know what you're doing. I have seen too many inexperienced principals get themselves in a hole because they try to work a small issue by themselves and eventually that small issue turns into a major problem that takes extensive school district resources to resolve. If they just asked for help in the beginning, they may have resolved the issue much more easily.

It is interesting that most superintendents spend the majority of their time working with principals who struggle to succeed in their jobs. However, I will add one more challenge to the leadership equation: Superintendents need to watch their most talented principals even closer.

Here is why. I am going to use a military story to demonstrate this point. I had a young commander working for me who was as good as they get. He had leadership skills, flying skills, and communication skills that everyone admired. He was the "Top Gun," as we would say, in most every level. But he was a partier. You can imagine his subordinates who admired him professionally would mimic his behavior because he was the leader everyone wanted to be. It is not always your most challenging subordinate you have to watch. Sometimes it is your best employee—a leader—who needs mentoring.

Watch the Monkeys on the Backs of New Leaders

As I noted earlier in this book, when a new leader assumed responsibility for a school, I often observed how they delegated in their new role and how they made the critical shift from being a doer to becoming a leader. In other fields of work, too, I would visit a new leader and ask to meet them in their new office. After some congratulations on their new position, I would ask them to take a walk around their entire building or buildings by themselves and then come back where I would be waiting for them in their office.

You can imagine the puzzlement. They would inevitably ask me about the purpose of this exercise, and I would say, "Please just do it and we will discuss it." Some were visibly annoyed because they had plenty to do beyond just walking around. After a while they would come back, still bewildered, and sit down with me. I would ask them to tell me who they talked with on the walk. They would list folks they had a conversation with, and, to come back to an anecdote I've mentioned before, I would ask them: "How many monkeys did you take off their backs?" That is, how many tasks did they put on themselves? (The term comes from the book *The One Minute Manager Meets the New Monkey.*) Inevitably, the new leader would list tasks they were asked to work on, perhaps a personnel issue, a scheduling issue, or a budget issue.

I then began to explain that that was not their job anymore and, if they took on all those tasks, they may not need all the people who worked for them since the new leader took the tasks away from their subordinates. I would explain that they were no longer a doer but needed to learn how to delegate and I would give them some advice on how to do it.

I learned from a mentor a long time ago that as a leader, I needed to work problems, but I needed to learn how to delegate. He gave me a three-step process that has saved me many times. First, when a subordinate comes to me with an issue, I ask them, "What is the problem?" We're looking to identify the problem itself, not the impact of the problem. Is it a personnel problem, a training problem, a budget issue, etc.?

Once that is cleared up, we move to the next question: "What are you doing to solve the problem?" As a leader, they have been given financial resources, legal options, or other tools to help resolve the issue to some extent even if they are limited. As a leader they should have tried to exhaust their skill set and resources, albeit limited, before coming to me.

The final question, when it is obvious that they have done all that they can do at their level, is to answer the question, "What do you suggest I do as your leader to help resolve the problem?" This is usually an eye-opener when they realize they should be asking that question before they come to the superintendent level. By delegating and using the whole team to work the issue, ideas can be generated and, when needed, presented for consideration at the superintendent level. This puts the monkey back on their backs, and they realize they have authority and responsibility to help solve the issue.

Delegation is an art and not a science and must be learned before you are an effective leader.

Communication

The toughest skill set to master is communication. It is a skill set you must continue to work on and must always work to grow. It can be argued you always strive for perfection but never master it, but you experience excellence along the way.

Remember the bag of sand metaphor I shared in Chapter Three? Well, getting information out to your organization is like passing a bag of sand up a scaffold. Contrary to common belief, the superintendent is not at the top but at the bottom of the scaffold struggling to raise the bag of sand that represents information to the next level. But the bag has a hole in it. The next person in the chain of command struggles to reach down and grab the bag to pass it up. And so it goes. When the bag gets to the newest person in the organization, there is no sand in it. The lesson is that communicating is not easy and you can't just depend on one manner of communication to get information out; you must work at communication in many forms.

Remember that story about the time posted a memo on bulletin boards with a $10 reward for the first person to read the communication and come to my office? It took more than three weeks to get a response! I definitely learned not to lean too heavily on a single means of communication.

As a supervisor, sometimes you need to gather information by burning some shoe leather. One night—yes, organizations work at night—I walked around the maintenance area where enlisted officers were inspecting an F-16 aircraft, and I saw they were working on the landing gear. I greeted them and asked how things were going. They said all was fine; they weren't going to open up to a senior officer that easily. I asked if I could help, and after an hour they told me that when they got off shift at 11 p.m. they would arrive at the chow hall and hot food was no longer being served. They also told me the washers and dryers weren't working well in the dormitories, and they told me about a discipline problem they were witnessing.

The next day I had my staff meeting with all the commanders and relayed this story. One of the commanders said, "Boss, if we had as many people working for us as you do, we would know about these issues." When I relayed these issues, I didn't say how I found out about these problems and, wouldn't you know it, those problems were in that squadron commander's outfit. You can't just depend on information bubbling up to the top all the time; sometimes you need to go out and get it.

Rules, Regulations, and Policies

As noted in an earlier section, it is always wise to revisit and examine your rules, regulations, and policies. What I found as a superintendent was that some of what was on our books hadn't been updated for decades. As a result, we did a six-month scrub of all the written guidance. We removed about one-quarter of the guidance, rewrote outdated regulations on more than half the guidance, republished directives that still were current, and added directives to match the times. Why this is important is very simple. If written directives are outdated or don't make sense for the times, people in the school district might conclude that they can selectively adhere to guidance and choose to follow only part of it.

Hiring and Firing

Hiring someone isn't easy. It takes time and effort to review applicants, interview the finalists, and negotiate an employment package. If not done diligently and the employee turns out to be a large challenge, the time spent on educating, advising, and maybe terminating them makes the hiring process look simple in comparison. The lesson is to take your time and never allow yourself to get in the position where you need to hire anyone breathing. You not only need to get the right people on the bus, but you also need to get them in the correct seats.

Firing someone is not easy, either. But when you find yourself, after a fair period of evaluation, making up for an employee's lack of ability, or if you're doing their job more than they are, it is time to make a change. Don't put it off. Bad news does not get better with time.

There are two kinds of firing: easy and hard. While it might sound counterintuitive, the easy firing occurs when an employee touches a child inappropriately, drives while drunk, or breaks another law. Although these are examples when someone may bring great discredit to the organization, it is relatively easy for the supervisor to make the decision, in most cases. The tougher firing is when you let someone go for lesser reasons and it is a judgment call. One way to do it, if able, is to let someone go and they don't know they have been fired. Let me explain. I have seen teachers who have been in the classroom too long. The front of their brain says they can't leave their students, while the back of the brain is screaming to get out of there. Moving someone with an offer to do something different (e.g., an administrative position, data management, coaching), allows the person to get a new perspective, and oftentimes they will thrive with a new challenge and keep their retirement pay. This may not be the way in all cases, but it can be a way.

Crisis Management

Leaders in school districts today must be trained on crisis management. As a leader in a school district, you have a hand receipt to ensure the safety and security of your staff and students, always. You need to be trained and actively practice exercises for circumstances such as natural disasters, medical emergencies, and shooters.

School supervisors need to lean forward. While it may not be the best analogy, it is easy to be in the back of a truck looking backward and keeping your head down. It is a lot harder to stand up in the back of the truck looking forward with your face in the wind anticipating what might and could happen and seeing what might be in front of you so you can avoid being jolted by branches or potholes in the road. Be proactive regarding safety, not reactive. Read the previous section on how you can establish an Incident Response Team. Through annual exercises with tough scenarios and deliberate debriefs, learn to be a crisis manager before there is a crisis.

Have you ever wondered how many issues are identified *after* a crisis? One reason is the inspectors after a serious incident go "freeze frame" in time. In other words, they can look back and examine every minute and every action in the comfort of detailed analysis over many weeks and months. As a leader, you don't have that luxury. But you can train your team with scenarios, building collaboration and trust, resulting in an experienced group of supervisors who have learned to think creatively, to be nimble, and to work together efficiently.

If you have ever seen the Blue Angels or the Thunderbirds fly, they are able to do those amazing things in the air because they debrief every flight with ultimate honesty and leave their egos at the door. While exercises aren't easy, the real value of learning is in a hotwash where everyone is brutally honest on what worked and what didn't work. As a superintendent, I really learned about my staff when we did exercises with thorough debriefs.

One trick of the trade is as follows: If you have an incident that thankfully did not result in a crisis, pull your team together and state that it did not result in a major accident but that you're going to do a mishap review as if it did actually result in a crisis. One time when I was a commander in a combat zone, I witnessed two aircraft that almost had a mid-air collision in the pattern after a mission but luckily did not. After I gave it some thought, I called my staff together and told them we would assume there was a mid-air and start an investigation. You would not believe the items we found wanting because we went freeze frame during that time sequence. While there was no wreckage and no one was hurt, we learned that the pilots were not current in some areas, the maintenance on the aircraft was not managed well in some respects, and the air traffic control that day had many flaws. All of this would have come out if there was really an accident. Without an accident, we wouldn't have found out any of that if we didn't do a hotwash on the simulated crisis scenario.

Quick Tips

- Lead by example, striving to do everything with class.
- Realize that if people ignore one standard, they're probably ignoring others, too.
- Work to make a team proud of the rules and apply all equally and fairly.
- Realize that when you disagree with someone, they may say you don't listen to them. Make sure you do listen, tell them you did listen, and, if you still do not agree, explain that.
- If you ever show anger publicly, make it planned and calculated, not emotional.
- Begin and end every conversation with students in mind; this helps prevent adult issues from getting in the way.

- If you could see a crisis you would have to deal with in the future, what books would you read? What mentors would you ask for? What preparations would you make? Continually learn with this attitude so you don't take the easier fork in the road when you shouldn't.
- Trust your instincts. You wouldn't be in a position of leadership if you hadn't already demonstrated good instincts along the way.
- Principals should look at least one year out, directors should look three years out, and superintendents should look five years out.
- Provide value. No matter who you are, what you do, or where you work, you want to be perceived as someone who provides value to the organization. When we talk about a personal leader brand, this is a significant component. If others question your value or wonder aloud what it is that you do for the organization, your perceived value is in jeopardy. To be successful, you want to be adding value.
- Live the values of the organization. The values of an organization are the mortar that holds the institution together.
- Be honest. The truth is a powerful, if often misunderstood, tool. Honesty isn't just the avoidance of lying, it's having the courage to tell the truth when others might not want to hear it. It's understanding that bad news isn't fine wine that gets better with age. And it's being

willing—and able—to be an honest broker when the situation calls for it.

- Be loyal. Trust and loyalty go hand in hand. Demonstrate loyalty, and you are likely to be seen as a trusted member of the organization. Violate that trust, and bad things happen. If you're going to be part of an organization, commit to the cause and give it your all. It will pay benefits beyond your imagination.

- Be humble. No matter who you are or where you go, there will always be someone else faster, stronger, smarter, and more talented. Never let your ego get in the way of being a valuable member of a bigger team. Never allow yourself to believe that you're always the smartest person in the room.

- Embrace risk. Nothing good comes from playing it safe all the time. Risk creates opportunities, which in turn brings value. If you really want to add value, you need to be comfortable with embracing risk.

- Be your best. Giving your best should be the status quo, but it's not. Many people find themselves just trying to keep up or trying to outperform someone else. To truly be your best, you want to challenge yourself, not anyone else. That means setting a bar that pushes you to your limits, then setting it again when you hit it. If you set that bar against someone else's performance, you'll never know for sure just how much you can do.

- Be a team player. As a member of an organization, you're a part of something bigger than you, part of a team, part of a family. Be positive, be proactive, be reliable. Support your other teammates and celebrate their accomplishments just as they support yours. Be that go-to person everyone trusts and admires.

- Be a change agent. Change is inevitable. You can either be part of the change or watch it pass you by. And if you continue to find yourself on the sidelines as a spectator in the crowd, you might want to revisit your value to the organization.
- Be unfailingly polite and professional. The moment you wade into a personal fight, you confer parity and legitimacy on your opponent—and risk embarrassing your own organization. And never hit "send" when you're angry, tired, or otherwise compromised.
- Time is the cup that measures the way. And truth be told, showing up is the truest recipe.
- Enjoy your job so your subordinates will look at you and want to aspire to your position.
- Leave it better than you found it.
- Be bold, decisive, and courageous with visions of fire for student success.

CHAPTER TWELVE

Key Insights and Takeaways

The transformative journey of K-12 school districts, exemplified by the case study of Aurora Public Schools (APS), underscores the profound impact of strategic leadership, inclusive planning, and unwavering commitment to implementation. This concluding chapter synthesizes the key insights from our transformative journey, underscores the importance of ownership as a catalyst for change, and aims to inspire educators, administrators, and stakeholders to embrace ownership in their own communities.

Key Insights and Takeaways

1. **Recognizing the Power of Nontraditional Educators.** One of the most valuable lessons from our journey is being open to integrating nontraditional educators into the leadership and strategic planning processes. These individuals often bring fresh perspectives and innovative solutions, identifying

obstacles that traditional educators might overlook. Their unique insights help illuminate the "rock in the road," enabling the development of more effective and comprehensive strategies for improvement.

2. **Strategic Planning and Vision Alignment.** Successful transformation hinges on clear, strategic planning that aligns vision with actionable goals and objectives. The APS experience highlighted the necessity of developing a concise, compelling vision—such as "Graduate every student with the choice to attend college, without remediation"—that inspires and guides the entire community. This vision, paired with a mission that details the organization's purpose and methods, provides a roadmap for sustained progress.

3. **Coalition Building and Community Involvement.** Building strong coalitions with community leaders, educators, parents, and students is essential. Engaging stakeholders through advisory councils and collaborative initiatives ensures that diverse perspectives are considered, fostering a sense of collective ownership and responsibility. This approach not only enriches the decision-making process but also strengthens community support and trust.

4. **Effective Communication.** Communication is critical to the success of any transformation initiative. Multiple communication channels—town hall meetings, surveys, social media, and more—ensure

that the vision and progress are clearly conveyed to all stakeholders. Innovative methods, such as incentivized memos, can enhance engagement and ensure the message reaches every corner of the organization.

5. **Data-Driven Decision-Making.** Using data to monitor progress and make informed decisions is vital. Transparent accountability systems, such as data walls and standards-based assessments, create a culture of mutual responsibility and continuous improvement. This data-driven approach helps identify areas of success and those needing further intervention, ensuring that strategies are adapted to meet evolving needs.

6. **Institutionalizing Change.** For change to be enduring, it must be institutionalized through updated policies and regulations. Reviewing and revising outdated policies ensures that the new approaches are formally embedded within the organizational framework, promoting consistency, fairness, and operational efficiency.

Ownership as a Catalyst for Meaningful Change

Ownership is the cornerstone of meaningful and sustainable transformation in K-12 education. When educators, administrators, students, and community members feel a sense of ownership over the educational process, they are more invested in its success. This sense of ownership fosters accountability, innovation, and a collective commitment to excellence. By empowering individuals at all levels to take initiative and contribute to the vision, we create a dynamic environment where positive change can thrive.

1. **Empowering Educators.** Empowering teachers and staff to take ownership of their professional development and instructional strategies leads to more engaged and motivated educators. When teachers are involved in decision-making processes and have the autonomy to innovate, they are more likely to implement effective teaching practices that enhance student learning.

2. **Engaging Students and Parents.** Students and parents who feel a sense of ownership over their educational experience are more likely to be actively involved and supportive. Encouraging student voice and choice in learning, as well as fostering strong partnerships between home and school, creates a supportive and inclusive educational environment.

Inspiring a Culture of Ownership and Excellence

The journey of transforming K-12 school districts is ongoing, and its success depends on the continuous pursuit of excellence through collective ownership. It is imperative to inspire readers to embrace this ethos within their own educational communities.

1. **Foster a Culture of Collaboration.** Encourage collaboration at all levels—among educators, between schools, and with the broader community. Collaborative efforts amplify strengths, address challenges collectively, and ensure that every voice is heard and valued.

2. **Commit to Continuous Improvement.** Transformation is not a one-time event but a continuous process. Commit to regularly reviewing and refining strategies, staying informed about best practices, and being open to new ideas and approaches. This commitment to continuous improvement will sustain momentum and drive long-term success.

3. **Lead by Example.** Leaders play a crucial role in modeling the behaviors and attitudes that promote ownership. By demonstrating transparency, accountability, and a genuine commitment to the vision, leaders can inspire others to take ownership and strive for excellence.

4. **Celebrate Successes and Learn from Failures.** Recognize and celebrate achievements, no matter how small, to build morale and reinforce the value of collective effort. Equally important is to learn from setbacks and view them as opportunities for growth and improvement.

As we move forward, let us remember that the power to transform education lies within each of us. By fostering a culture of ownership, collaboration, and continuous improvement, we can create educational environments where each student has the opportunity to succeed and thrive. Let this journey of transformation inspire and guide us toward a future of excellence in K-12 education for the students, always the students!

Superintendent Ninety-Day Listening Tour

Immediate Mandate

The school district is in the middle of a transformational change. The new superintendent has an immediate and moral mandate to raise student achievement and close the achievement gap between ethnic groups and between economically disadvantaged and economically advantaged students. To that end, the superintendent must:

- Build on the work to date and impart a sense of urgency with a coherent vision and strategic plan for school improvement.
- Convey a positive public image of the district.
- Engage stakeholders from across the district and economic strata in reciprocal accountability.

- Oversee the recruitment and hiring of a highly qualified, diverse workforce.
- Serve as the district's most vocal promoter and supporter.

Rationale for Entry Plan

This document serves as an Entry Plan for the first ninety days, including meetings with key leaders and stakeholders. However, as the ninety-day period progresses, the superintendent reserves the right to make modifications to the plan as conversations with stakeholders progress. This protocol allows flexibility in planning while offering a systematic plan of action for conceptualizing the district's current challenges and future vision.

Organization of District Leadership

Within the initial ninety-day period, the superintendent will always focus on the key goal of accelerating student achievement and do the following:

- Work with the board in agreeing to develop a strategic plan for the district.
- Identify and establish clarity of roles between the board, the superintendent, and each of the key district stakeholders.
- Review and adjust the building blocks of reform governance such as board meetings, workshops, committees,

and administrative support, with the approval of
the board.

- Review and adjust policy development and oversight in
coordination with the board.
- Build civic capacity and transition planning.
- At the end of the ninety-day period, deliver to the board
for approval a revised vision and strategic plan.

Ninety-Day Entry Plan: Goals, Objectives, and Key Activities

Goal 1: Effective Governance (Board–Superintendent)

Objectives

- Operate as a cohesive leadership team with a student-centered agenda.
- Build positive, professional relationships with each board member.

Key Activities

- Hold an off-site board retreat (roles, norms, accountability).

- Meet regularly with the Board president; schedule 1:1s with all members.
- Establish a simple cadence for updates (e.g., weekly brief).
- Launch a timeline to refresh vision, mission, beliefs, and performance measures.

Goal 2: Student Achievement (Instruction and Support)

Objectives

- Use data to identify achievement patterns and close gaps.
- Raise expectations for all students.
- Monitor, evaluate, and improve instructional supports.

Key Activities

- Conduct an academic audit of curriculum, instruction, and materials.
- Review achievement by subgroup; run basic cross-tabs to spot gaps.
- Increase graduation rates; expand advanced placement, dual credit, internships, and research.
- Check scope/sequence and assessments for rigor, standards alignment, and supports for English learners and students with disabilities.
- Build a by-student/by-school participation dashboard for interventions and track outcomes.

Goal 3: Public Trust & Communication

Objectives

- Understand the community—culture, history, expectations.
- Strengthen partnerships with civic, faith, and community organizations.
- Communicate clearly and consistently; build advocacy and media relations.

Key Activities

- Map key leaders (business, foundations, public safety, higher ed, faith).
- Meet priority stakeholders; attend major civic forums; host biannual roundtables.
- Review all channels (staff, families, partners, policymakers) and simplify formats.
- Meet the editorial board; host a media meet-and-greet; invite press to key events.
- Tell the district story—regular updates tied to vision, mission, and results.

Goal 4: Organizational Effectiveness and Efficiency

Objectives

- Assess where we are and where we need to go in every division.

- Streamline structures, roles, and processes to better serve schools.

Key Activities

- Review org chart, policies, handbooks, studies, and school-level data.
- Hold division reviews (start/stop/continue; support needed; quick fixes).
- Set timelines for a strategic plan, facilities plan, and long-range tech plan.
- Reorganize central services for school-first delivery; align funding to schools.
- Establish quarterly metrics and a simple accountability scorecard.

Goal 5: Climate and Culture

Objectives

- Build trust with leaders, staff, and schools; recognize every role.
- Engage parents as partners.
- Maintain constructive labor relations.
- Coordinate with city and state leaders on student priorities.

Key Activities

- Visit every department and school; hold monthly "teacher coffees."

- Host PTO presidents; create regular family forums and feedback loops.
- Meet union leaders; set monthly touchpoints and a mini-retreat (roles and norms).
- Meet the mayor/council, commissioner of education, legislative delegation, and federal representatives; establish a steady advocacy cadence.

Goal 6: Student Achievement (Deep Dive)
Objective

- Drive measurable gains through targeted audits, rigor, and monitoring.

Key Activities

- Inventory instructional tech and software; track who uses what and with what results.
- Evaluate each intervention's impact; keep/scale what works, sunset what doesn't.
- Publish a simple "achievement gains" update each quarter.

Goal 7: Governance in Action (Board–Superintendent Operations)
Objective

- Clarify roles and mutual accountability; keep governance student-focused.

- Key Activities
- Finalize retreat outputs (role clarity, agenda standards, decision protocols).
- Align board calendars, committee work, and data displays to student outcomes.
- Standardize agenda memos and consent items; minimize surprises.

Goal 8: Community Relationships and Advocacy

Objectives

- Broaden ownership of student success across the whole community.
- Convert partners into advocates for key goals.

Key Activities

- Convene cross-sector partners twice a year; publish shared commitments.
- Track partner contributions (time, talent, treasure) against student outcomes.
- Provide talking points and "how to help" toolkits for business, faith, and civic groups.

Goal 9: Systems, People, and Resources

Objectives

- Align people, processes, and dollars to what moves student learning.

- Reduce duplication; improve turnaround time and service quality.

Key Activities

- Conduct a service map (who does what; for whom; how fast; with what result).
- Redesign workflows; consolidate overlapping roles/units.
- Create a funding alignment plan that shifts resources closest to students.
- Report quarterly on service metrics and corrective actions.

Goal 10: Welcoming, High-Performing District

Objectives

- Ensure every interaction reflects respect, urgency, and professionalism.
- Make families and staff feel seen, supported, and accountable for results.

Key Activities

- Establish simple norms for meetings, email, response times, and follow-through.
- Launch a "leaders in schools" schedule: principals, cabinet, and central staff in buildings weekly.

- Recognize excellence (staff, students, partners) in every public meeting.
- Close the loop: Share what was heard, what was done, and what's next.

Ninety-Day Stakeholder Interviews and Timelines

Board of Education

Purpose: Establish working relationships with individual board members and the key stakeholders as a whole.

PRIOR TO START DATE

Facilitate and co-plan a board retreat:

1. Establish mutual expectations.
2. Agree on communication expectations.
3. Review the governance team history and ground rules.
4. Outline the Entry Plan.

5. Discuss immediate issues of concern (e.g., staff going around the superintendent to the board is not acceptable).
6. Establish board/superintendent performance expectations and appraisal (with examples).

30 DAYS

Hold individual interview sessions with each board member and invite each board member and their partner to dinner at a restaurant in the board member's district. Potential topics of discussion:

- Autobiographical information and organizations they belong to
- History of the board
- General impressions of the schools and teaching staff
- Perceptions of strengths and weaknesses of the administrative staff
- Key issues the district must face and why, ranked in priority order
- People in the schools or community who try to influence school issues
- What needs to be preserved/changed with the district
- Type of leadership provided by the superintendent
- Level of satisfaction with how the board works as a group

60 DAYS

Hold a session with the board chairperson to discuss roles, procedures, and working relationships. Potential topics:

- Board agendas
- Internal/external communication and confidentiality
- A schedule for regular review and planning sessions
- Establish weekly meetings with the board chairperson

Schedule sessions to review information from previous interviews and draft an initial action plan to address any issues that came up concerning the operation of the board.

90 DAYS

Follow-up session with the board to present any changes to district personnel and operations based upon the input gathered from all other groups:

- Share preliminary findings with the board
- Present and agree on plan of action for year 1
- Review communication needs, channels, and expectations
- Discuss how potential problems will be addressed
- Review the superintendent's expectations for them

District Senior Staff/Central Office

Purpose: Establish strong professional relationships with key personnel inside the district.

30 DAYS

A. Conduct a session with the superintendent's office (e.g., secretary, clerk of board) to establish office procedures/communication.

    1. Data immersion:

        a. Board policy manual and administrative procedure guide

        b. Board meeting minutes for past year

        c. Student achievement data

        d. Curriculum

        e. District and building-level plans

        f. Audits for last three years

        g. District marketing and communications plan

B. Hold a series of meetings with the outgoing superintendent (if possible) to obtain relevant information on district history.

C. "Meet and greet" tour of the central office facility to be introduced to staff, including directors, secretaries, and custodians. Schedule an informal reception for additional communication opportunities.

D. Conduct briefing/interview sessions with key cabinet and central office staff members. Priority sessions with Curriculum and Finance personnel:

    1. Potential interview questions:

- Autobiographical information/resume
- Areas of responsibility (individual and shared)
- Key issues for their responsibilities to the district/major decisions to be made within the next ninety days
- School district's key issues
- People who try to influence school issues
- What needs to be preserved or changed within the district
- Type of leadership provided by the superintendent in the past—what is expected in the future

2. Establish how communication and decision-making will occur between each department and the superintendent, the board, the community, and the district's internal audiences.
3. Determine regular meeting schedules when appropriate.

60–90 DAYS

Conduct follow-up sessions within a month of the briefing sessions with key cabinet and central office staff (individually or in small groups) to review information gathered from briefings and interviews. Establish six-month work plan for predictable tasks.

District Tour/School Unit Leadership

Purpose: Be a visible presence to the staff in the district.

FIRST DAY ON THE JOB

All staff meeting and a introductory speech—a superintendent makes both technical and symbolic decisions. Nothing is more symbolic than how a superintendent spends the first day on the job. This speech will outline the focus for the next ninety days, and arrangements will be made for visible activities supporting that focus.

FIRST DAY OF SCHOOL

Ride a bus in one of the poorest areas and greet and talk to kids as they get on, then visit their school and a couple of others that morning.

30 DAYS

A. Establish all-administrative sessions with all key district stakeholders (principals, teachers, staff, parents, and the public) to outline goals for the first ninety days. Schedule a series of ninety-minute meetings with these groups, telling them their district can be the best in the state in five years, that we have a great base to build upon and that we all need to work together. Two questions will be asked: What do we have going for us now? And what are the barriers? Use brainstorming and multi-voting. Allow time for questions and answers.

B. Request a binder of resumes from the Personnel office for the top fifty district staff positions.

C. Request briefing papers from the staff on critical issues areas—budget, litigation, data information systems, and technology—and any recent reorganizations or audits. For each, ask senior staff to describe the district's current situation and ask what major decisions need to be made in one month, three months, and six months.

D. Hold breakfasts offsite with four or five senior district staff members each week.

    1. Distribute a letter to staff members outlining immediate goals.

    2. After the first week on the job, begin visiting schools. Arrange a highly visible helicopter or driving tour of the district's boundaries with the mayor, the police chief, and other notable community, business, and religious leaders.

E. Visit various local communities with the individual school board member who represents that area of the city.

F. Each day, visit schools, including nontraditional schools such as charter or special education, and district field offices.

G. Attend at least one faculty meeting at each school during the year.

H. Start the year-long process of attending extracurricular school events.

60 DAYS

Arrange meetings by grade level (elementary, middle school, and high school) to obtain knowledge of issues relevant at each level.

1. Prior to the meeting, obtain resume information for each principal, including most recent evaluations.
2. Meet with central office administrators responsible for principal evaluations to interpret data collected on the principals.

60-90 DAYS

After sixty days, meet with principals and evaluators to establish work plans in line with district needs.

Union Leadership

Purpose: Establish relationships with the district's labor union and professional associations.

30 DAYS

A. Meet with appropriate Human Resources personnel to get background regarding union/management relationships. Form a strategy for working with each group.

B. Meet individually with the leadership of each employee group within the first thirty days. Meet with the heads of the teacher, administrator, classified, police, and other unions. Establish a regular communication pattern with union leaders. Consider writing an article for each union paper. Potential topics at meetings:

- Autobiographical information on each leader
- Key issues the district faces from the perspective of the union (ranked in priority order)
- Describe the history of the union/administration/ board relationships
- What worked well/needs to change regarding communication with the superintendent? Unresolved contract issues
- Perspective on the effectiveness of district leadership

60 DAYS

Within sixty days, have a follow-up session to review work plans based upon the information obtained during the first session.

90 DAYS

Establish regular communication channels. (The superintendent may not necessarily meet with the groups each time.)

Community Leadership

Purpose: To meet leaders of community and parent organizations, generate good will, build support, and establish critical communication channels.

Continue all year. Ask each board member for three to five names of organization leaders, and have the school board arrange meetings. Arrange a series of speaking engagements with business organizations such as:

- Chamber of Commerce
- Rotary groups
- Corporate councils
- Educational foundations
- Kiwanis clubs
- Urban League

30 DAYS

Hold community meetings sponsored by the parent group in each of the high schools for the parents of the geographic area around each high school. Meet with the superintendents of any surrounding school districts to determine common issues and establish communication channels.

60 DAYS

Meet with major community organizations to review the status of their relationship with the district:

- Junior Achievement
- Urban League
- National Association for the Advancement of Colored People (NAACP)
- Hispanic support groups
- Any other group representing the interest of minority populations within the district

- United Way
- Representatives from local faith-based organizations
- Local colleges and universities

Review any previous program collaborations and lay the groundwork for future efforts.

Meet with the representatives from the social service agencies that provide services to the families in the district. Begin an assessment of the effectiveness of the collaborations between the school and the district.

90 DAYS

Develop a strategic plan for maximizing the district's connections to the community groups.

Political Leadership

Purpose: Meet political power brokers and establish regular communication. All timelines depend on whether legislative sessions are occurring at the start of the new superintendent's term.

30–60 DAYS

Local:

- Meet with the district's legal counsel to review the district's lobbying efforts at the local, state, and national levels.

- Meet with the mayor and the city council members to gain their support for the goals of the district. If the district is not contiguous within a single city, meet some of the other mayors whose cities are part of the district's boundaries.
- Begin developing a work plan that will address gaps in the current efforts, and provide focus to the next legislative sessions.
- Ask the district's legal counsel to develop a primer on state education code, paying particular attention to statutes currently impacting or likely to impact the district.

60 DAYS

State:

- Meet the governor and the state's chief school officer. Bring the school board president, one or two senior staff members, and union leadership.
- Investigate the district's involvement in any state superintendent, administrative, and education associations and strengthen the district's involvement with these organizations.
- Meet with the leadership of the district's unions, the local Chamber of Commerce, and parent organizations to coordinate lobbying efforts.

90 DAYS

National:

- Update the status of the district's membership in national educational associations to tap into their legislative agendas.
- Meet with the congressional representatives and senators for the district.

Media

Purpose: Clearly articulate the vision of the district so that the public, press, and education community know what to expect.

30 DAYS

- Within the first week on the job, have the district's Communications office organize a news conference for all media organizations. Conduct as many one-on-one interviews as feasible and invite media to community sessions when appropriate. If entering a district with a majority Latino student population, consider hiring a district press officer who is bilingual.
- Meet with all local newspaper editorial boards, being sure to include multicultural and business-focused press.
- Develop a short camera-ready message to parents to be included in school newsletters.

- Update the district's website to include a message and biographical information about the new superintendent.
- Work with the Communications department to develop an informal half-hour "Meet the New Superintendent" TV presentation for the district's educational channel.

National Leadership

Purpose: Take the story of the district's strategic plan to key political, foundation, and education leaders in the city, state, and across the country.

- Visit Washington, DC (with local mayor) to meet with that city's DC delegation, the White House, the Council of Great City Schools, leaders in the Department of Education, and others who can be helpful in providing resources and technical assistance to the district.
- Invite national foundation presidents to visit once the district is ready to ask for philanthropic resources to assist with its strategic priorities.
- Tap into network of education organization leaders to assist with district's strategic priorities and to bring fresh talent and expertise to any district that has traditionally been very parochial in its outreach efforts.

- Consider taking advantage of the Broad Foundation's "Strategic Support Teams" initiative (spend a closed-door, working weekend with highly regarded urban superintendents from across the country).

Incident Response Team Checklists

Checklist for Superintendent or Chief Operating Officer

The superintendent or chief operating officer is the only position that must be filled at all times. The deputy superintendent will be primary/backup, as directed by the superintendent.

Immediately establish contact via telecommunications and webinar with key agencies/districts involves.

Establish contact with police department, fire department, and liaison directors on the scene. If this is an exercise, preface all comments on phones with "This is an exercise."

1. Monitor roll call to ensure correct Incident Response Team (IRT) participants are in attendance.

2. Confirm participation for the teleconference and identify participants.
3. Using Global Information Systems, identify district facilities in 1, 2 or 3 miles of the incident.
4. Use wall maps in the Emergency Operations Center to determine the perimeter within a one-, three-, or five-mile radius of the incident location.
5. Establish objectives/outcomes.
6. For a big-picture view, make an information board and keep it up to date.
7. Identify potentially impacted staff and students and consider facility lockdowns for affected sites.
8. Receive initial briefs from Security, School Services, Communication, Transportation, HR, Medical, Weather, and Legal.
9. Get updated information from local authorities and liaison director (chief of security or their deputy) who is at the scene.
10. Ensure communication protocol is established by the police department's public information officer.
    a. Call to board of education
    b. Press release prepared and coordinated with public information officer
    c. Call to principals, schools, and sites of interest
    d. Call to staff
    e. Call to families

11. Delegate tasks to IRT as necessary and ensure checklists are being followed.
12. Post a security guard at entry to the IRT to monitor who comes and goes from the suite.
13. Consider releasing/holding IRT members who are not directly needed for the incident. Or, if the incident requires multiple days, set up an evening team so the day team can rest.
14. Get building schematics as necessary.
15. Bring up building cameras as necessary to view areas of interest.
16. Monitor television telecasts that may be covering the incident; be prepared to record news telecasts for future review as needed.
17. Connect with Zonar (commercial bus tracking system) and consider freezing all buses to ensure vehicles do not enter containment areas or exit containment areas without a police escort, as necessary. Put three buses on alert for evacuation movement as necessary.
18. Establish parent reunification site by notifying the respective school and deploy crisis counselors to the site.
19. Brief IRT members hourly with updated information using briefing slides.
20. Send incident log to police/fire departments every 15–30 minutes.

21. Always monitor buildings on lockdown and release as necessary.
22. Always monitor the weather.
23. Consider cancelling school at affected locations that have activities for that day and other days as necessary.
24. Fax/scan/email/hand-deliver information on students and employees (e.g., pictures, medical information) as necessary.
    a. Information to assist on hostage negotiations
    b. Information to help police distinguish suspects from innocent people
    c. Account for personnel and ensure all are evacuated to a safe location as soon as possible
    d. Use a whiteboard to list the names and photos of anyone not accounted for; remove as necessary as they are accounted for
    e. Assist police with a person familiar with the area (e.g., custodian) who can see if there is anything out of place
25. Food services provide food as necessary.
26. Consider 24-hour operations and work shifts with alternate IRT members.
27. Work after incident contingency plan:
    a. Maintenance and operational cleanup
    b. Press conference

    c. Crisis Action Team plan for dealing with affected students (involved students, friends, siblings) or employees

    d. Plan for opening schools and how to do it

    e. Consider memorial services if needed

28. Ensure after action report is completed.

29. Establish a webinar with key players as needed.

Incident Response Team Checklist for Public Affairs/PIO

BACKUP: DEPUTY

* Report to the IRT with a laptop
* Contact local emergency agencies: Joint Information Center
* Assist in drafting external messages, i.e., email, website, etc.
* Oversee media response
* Perform tasks as assigned by incident commander

IN ADVANCE (WHEN POSSIBLE):

Draft the following:

* Media release
* Talking points and fact sheets
* Web items
* Telephone scripts
* Letters in English and Spanish (or other common language in the district)
* Emails
* Media passes

Contact department players as needed:

* Administrative team turn on news broadcast and begin taping

- Confirm understanding of issue
- Staff and students involved
- Impacted sites
- Available resources (e.g., phones, computers, power)
- Timelines: Who has been contacted at this point (e.g., parents, other staff, IRT, superintendent, board of education)?

CALM-PLAN BEFORE ACTING:

- Assign a reality checker to assess our work and plans
- Support teammates
- Plan breaks, and don't be afraid to ask for more breaks if pressure is getting to you
- Plan for the long haul, how to relieve each other, provide refreshments, and support needs
- Be sensitive to others who may have family working in or attending our schools

Determine who will:

- Go to the site
- Go to command center
- Research additional facts
- Locate applicable district policies and regulations
- Assess translation/interpretation needs
- Assess print service needs
- Assist with office phones
- Provide phone script(s)

- Verify that DVDs are recording
- Finalize communication and determine appropriate audiences
- Communication tools (in conjunction with others on IRT, especially legal counsel)
- Finalize media release
- Finalize talking points and fact sheets
- Finalize web items
- Finalize telephone scripts
- Finalize letters
- Finalize emails
- Translate/interpret above items as needed
- Determine appropriate audiences

  - Internal: superintendent, board, leadership team, administration building receptionist, affected site staff, general staff, bus drivers, communications team
  - Partner audiences: students, parents, key communicator network (city council, elected officials, District Accountability Board, Foundation Board, key community and business groups and general subscribers), other public information officers (e.g., police, fire, city, health), media, state professional communication organization

- Assess additional audiences and communication tools needed

- Visit hospitals as needed (coordinate with crisis debriefing team)
- News conferences:

    - Coordinate events and statements with other agencies (e.g., police, fire, city)
    - Schedule time, date, and location
    - Heads up to IRT, leadership team, and board of education
    - Distribute media release announcing conference
    - Prepare and rehearse all spokespersons (provide media preparation handouts and talking points)

- Prepare fact sheets for distribution

    - Create and distribute media passes
    - Distribute fact sheets to media attendees
    - Conduct conference

- Debrief and follow-up

    - Assess communication effectiveness
    - Review media coverage and debrief with spokespeople
    - Determine if additional communication is needed (short- and long-term)
    - Have communication team conduct lessons learned session

Incident Response Team Checklist for Chief Academic Officer

INSTRUCTIONAL EXPERT
Backup: As Assigned
1. Report to IRT with laptop.
2. Provide information on school contact days.
3. Inform IRT of any pertinent State Department of Education information.
4. Provide information on school start and end times and evening events that could be affected by the incident.
5. Advise alternative educational options to continue the educational process.
6. Perform tasks as assigned by incident commander.
7. Inform appropriate members of the Division of Instruction to be on call for the duration of the incident.
8. Work with the Communications team in getting a list of any held/injured students and work with family communication.

Incident Response Team Checklist for Chief Legal Counsel

Backup: District External Legal Advisors

1. Report to Crisis Command Center.
2. Assist with school liaison in communicating key facts and information to the board of education and superintendent.
3. Provide legal advice to incident commander, superintendent, and board of education on incident-related items.
4. Provide legal advice on preservation of evidence and identification of witnesses and facilitate the protection of attorney-client privilege.
5. Assist in establishing appropriate coordination between district investigation and law enforcement investigation into the incident.
6. Participate in follow-up meetings at the involved site to determine facts and assess exposure to liability.
7. Participate in review of press releases and written communications to parents and guardians.
8. Assist Risk Management Office in ensuring insurance carriers are alerted to potential claims.

Incident Response Team Checklist for Hazardous Response Individual

OIL AND HAZARDOUS MATERIALS
Backup: Deputy

Provide information about hazardous materials involved in an accident. Provide pertinent information about storage locations of hazardous materials, chemical inventories, material safety data sheets, hazards, appropriate response actions, and reporting requirements. If structural building damage is involved, also provide information about the location and appropriate cleanup of asbestos building material:

- Report to the IRT Room with a laptop, two-way radio, cell phone, and personal identification.
- Access hazardous storage records.
- Ensure access to building management plans that speak to asbestos exposures.
- Access inventory for science lab information if needed.
- Prepare vendor list to obtain personal protective equipment.
- Post student/staff photos and information on side wall as required.
- Perform tasks as assigned by the incident commander.

Hazardous Materials

- Determine whether people are in the immediate area and associated injuries related to spill.
- Determine what material spilled.
- Determine type of hazard.
- Determine location and quantity of spill.
- Determine if spill is a threat to human health and/or the environment:

  - Cross-reference chemical inventory for area to assess additional hazards present.
  - Determine if spilled materials can react with stored chemicals in immediate area.
  - Determine if reportable quantity spilled and notify corresponding agencies.
  - Determine if minor or major spill, can it be mitigated by district personnel or if outside contractor is necessary.
  - Contact appropriate contractor if necessary.
  - Complete local, state, and federal requirements.
  - Consult with medical experts regarding blood pathogen requirements.

Structural damage to a building:

- Determine if building materials contain asbestos.
- Determine the locations and buildings involved.
- Determine whether it is a major or minor contamination.

- Determine if evacuation is necessary.
- Determine whether an outside contractor is needed for mitigation.
- Contact appropriate contractor, if necessary.
- Determine if a reportable quantity spilled and, if necessary, notify the State Department of Health and Environment and Air Pollution Control Division. Follow up with a written report, if needed.

Incident Response Team Checklist for Chief of Food Services

Backup: As Assigned

- Assess employee injuries for any nutrition requirements.
- Immediately communicate with supervisors and maintain communication throughout entire incident.
- Gather employees from other sites to a central location dependent on emergency for beginning food preparation for students, staff, rescue workers, etc.
- Create an employee schedule using the data received from the command center.
- Prepare boxed food as needed.
- Deliver food to a predetermined safe feeding location.
- Deliver food to emergency workers as police allow.
- Record all food used, including snacks, and a count of meals served.
- Assist with food distribution for city police and fire department as needed and able.
- If specific schools close, move food to open schools as needed.
- Move employees to other sites as schools close or as attendance drops.
- Notify vendors and keep vendors posted regarding district needs.
- Work with surrounding school districts' nutrition service departments as necessary.

- Work with custodians to clean all tables after breakfast and between each group of students at lunch.
- If students have meals in their classroom, ensure that cleaning materials are provided to each classroom with the assistance of custodians.
- Track all costs associated with the incident.

APPENDIX E

Resources

Aurora Public Schools. "2006–2007 Annual Report Card," Colorado Department of Education, https://www.cde.state.co.us/.

Black, Alexis-Gonzales, and Kim Anthony. *The New School Rules: 6 Vital Practices for Thriving and Responsive Schools.* Corwin Publishers, 2018.

Blanchard, Ken, William Oncken Jr., and Hal Burrows. *The One Minute Manager Meets the Monkey.* William Morrow, 1989.

Buchanan, Bruce. *Turnover at the Top: Leadership Instability in America's Largest School Districts.* Teachers College Press, 2006.

Carver, John, and Miriam Carver. *Reinventing Your Board: A Step-by-Step Guide to Implementing Policy Governance.* Jossey-Bass, 1997.

Carver, John, with Caroline Olive. *Corporate Boards That Create Value: Governing Company Performance from the Boardroom.* Jossey-Bass, 2002.

Carver, John. *Boards That Make a Difference: A New Design for Leadership in Nonprofit and Public Organizations.* Jossey-Bass, 2006.

Carver, John. *John Carver on Board Leadership: Selected Writings from the Creator of the World's Most Provocative and Systematic Governance Model.* Jossey-Bass, 2001.

Columbia Accident Investigation Board, August 2003. Government Printing Office, 2003. https://www.nasa.gov/columbia/home/CAIB_Vol1.html

Devens, Jeff. *School Crisis Survival Guide: Management Techniques and Materials for Counselors and Administrators.* Free Spirit Publishing, 2004.

Johnston, Peter H. *Choice Words: How Our Language Affects Children's Learning.* Stenhouse Publishers, 2004.

Kotter, John P. *Leading Change: Why Transformation Efforts Fail.* Harvard Business Review Press, 2007.

Kowalski, Theodore J. *Effective Communication for District and School Administrators.* Rowman & Littlefield, 2005.

Krantz, Gene. *Failure Is Not an Option: Mission Control from Mercury to Apollo 13 and Beyond.* Berkley Books, 2009.

Mahbubani, Kishmore. *The Great Convergence: Asia, the West, and the Convergence of One World.* Public Affairs, 2012.

McAdams, Don R. *What School Boards Can Do.* Teachers College Press, 2006.

Stanford, John. *Victory in Our Schools: We Can Give Our Children Excellent Public Education*. Bantam Books, 1999.

Vaughn, Diane. *The Challenger Launch Decision: Risky Technology, Culture, and Deviance at NASA*. University of Chicago Press, 1996.

Williamson, Ronald, and Barbara Blackburn, *Hiring and Firing the Best Staff for Your School*. Routledge, 2009.

About the Author

John L. Barry, Major General, USAF (Ret) is chairman of the Air Force Historical Society and vice chair of the National Aviation Hall of Fame. From 2017 to 2025, he served as President and CEO of the Wings Over the Rockies Air & Space Museum (WOTR), Colorado's Official Air and Space Museum. In 2018, WOTR was recognized by CNN as one of the top 20 Aviation Museums in the World and by *USA Today* as one of the top 10 Museums in the United States. As president and CEO of the Boys & Girls Clubs of Metro Denver (BGCMD) from 2014 to 2016, John was responsible for 2,000 kids each day with 10,000 members, 225 full- and part-time staff, and a $16 million annual budget.

John served as Superintendent of Aurora Public Schools for seven years, from 2006 to 2013, leading sixty schools and 40,000 students and overseeing a $500 million budget. His team instituted Concurrent Enrollment in 2008 (college credit in the APS High Schools), which then spread across the nation.

Before returning to Colorado, John served in the United States Air Force for over 30 years as a combat veteran with 270 hours of combat time, fighter pilot, Fighter Weapons School Graduate, winning team member at the "Top Gun" international Air-to-Air William Tell Competition, Military Assistant to the Secretary of Defense, and commander multiple times at the Squadron level, twice at the Group Command level, and twice at the Wing Command level. He is also a survivor of the 9/11 attack on the Pentagon while serving as the lead Strategic Planner for the United States Air Force. He retired in 2004 as a Major General and finished his USAF career as board member and Executive Director of the Space Shuttle Columbia Accident Investigation.

John is a 1973 honor graduate of the United States Air Force Academy with a double major in International Affairs and Political Science and a distinguished graduate of USAF Pilot Training. He earned a master's degree in Public Administration from Oklahoma University, was a White House Fellow from 1986 to 1987, attended the Kennedy School of Government at Harvard on a fellowship from 1993 to 1994, and is a 2004 graduate of the Broad Superintendents Academy.

In 2011, John was selected by the Colorado Association of School Executives as the Colorado Superintendent of the Year—the first nontraditional Superintendent in Colorado to be chosen. He was recognized with a Lifetime Achievement Award from the Colorado Aviation Historical Society in 2021; awarded the Annual Colorado Space Business Coalition Cosmic Contributor Award in 2022; and inducted into the Titan 100 CEOs Hall of Fame in Colorado, inducted into the Colorado Aviation Hall of Fame, and honored by the Denver Business Journal as a Most Admired CEO in 2023. He was awarded the White House Presidential Lifetime Achievement Award for volunteer services in 2024.

www.ingramcontent.com/pod-product-compliance
Lightning Source LLC
Chambersburg PA
CBHW062119020426
42335CB00013B/1020